Lifescripts

Also by Stephen M. Pollan and Mark Levine

Lifescripts: What to Say to Get What You Want in 101 of Life's Toughest Situations

Surviving the Squeeze

The Total Negotiator

The Big Fix-Up: Renovating Your Home Without Losing Your Shirt

The Business of Living

Your Recession Handbook: How to Thrive and Profit During Hard Times

The Field Guide to Starting a Business

The Field Guide to Home Buying in America

Lifescripts
for Managers

Introduction by Stephen M. Pollan

Written by:

Mark Levine, Michael Caplan, Jonathon Epps,
Andrew Frothingham, Erik Kolbell, Deirdre Martin,
William Martin, Nick Morrow, Allison Noel,
Aldo Pascarella, and Roni Beth Tower

Macmillan • USA

MACMILLAN GENERAL REFERENCE USA
A Pearson Education Macmillan Company
1633 Broadway
New York, NY 10019-6785

Macmillan Publishing books may be purchased for business or sales promotional use.
For information please write: Special Markets Department, Macmillan Publishing USA,
1633 Broadway, New York, NY 10019.

Book Design by Nick Anderson

Library of Congress Cataloging-in-Publication Data

Lifescripts for Managers / introduction by Stephen M. Pollan : written
by Mark Levine . . . [et al.].
        p.   cm.
    Includes index.
    ISBN 0-02-862622-2
    1. Business communication. 2. Interpersonal communication.
3. Executives.   I. Pollan, Stephen M.   II. Levine, Mark,   1958–
HF5718.L52 1999
658.4'5—dc21   98-52415
                                                                   CIP

Manufactured in the United States of America
10 9 8 7 6 5 4 3 2 1

CONTENTS

I'm the first to admit I don't know everything. I'm always turning to others to fill gaps in my own expertise. So when I was asked to put together this follow-up to *Lifescripts,* I knew that to dig deeper into the world of workplace communications and come back with original, creative, and pragmatic new material I'd need help. In response, I was lucky enough to be able to put together a team of outstanding lifescript authors, each with his or her own unique qualifications, expertise, and approach.

Mark Levine is a writer and editor who has collaborated with Stephen Pollan on fourteen books, including the original *Lifescripts* and their recent best–selling contrarian looks at spending and earning money, *Die Broke* (HarperCollins, 1997) and *Live Rich* (HarperCollins, 1998). His work has also appeared in a variety of publications including *Worth, New York, Money,* and *Working Woman.* He has taught magazine writing at Cornell University and lectured at the Newhouse School at Syracuse University; his articles have twice been nominated for National Magazine Awards. He lives in Ithaca, New York.

Michael Caplan is a freelance writer who lives in New York City. He is currently working in script development with Borracho Pictures.

Jonathon Epps is a sales and marketing consultant. He is the owner of The Selling Source, Inc., a consulting firm specializing in architectural specification sales and marketing and professional development. He lives in Ithaca, New York, with his wife, JoAnn Cornish–Epps, and their two children, Paula and Sam.

Andrew Frothingham is a Manhattan–based consultant and freelance writer specializing in business communications, including speeches, newsletters, training films, and inspirational T-shirts. He has written, co–written, and ghost–written numerous reference and humor books. He became a full–time writer after careers as a teacher, researcher, advertising executive, and high-tech marketer. He earned two degrees from Harvard and is now in the process of being re–educated by his young son.

Erik Kolbell is a graduate of Brown University, Yale Divinity School, and the University of Michigan. An ordained Congregational minister, Kolbell has served in university and church settings. He is also a licensed psychotherapist practicing in New York City. He has written articles for numerous publications including *Newsweek, The New York Times, Parents,* and *Child.*

Deirdre Martin is a full–time freelance writer and member of both the American Society of Journalists and Authors and the Writer's Guild of America. Her work has appeared in a wide variety of publications, including *New Woman, McCall's, Seventeen, YM, Fitness, Bride's, Modern Maturity,* and *InsideSports.* She is the author of *The Real Life Guide to Investing for Retirement* (Avon, 1998) and has written for the daytime drama "One Life to Live."

William Martin spent more than three decades as a high school teacher and associate principal having dialogues with students, teachers, administrators, building staff, and parents. He is now a freelance writer and educational consultant. He lives with his wife, Barbara, in Northport, New York.

Nick Morrow is a tax accountant practicing with Martin Geller CPA in New York City and specializes in advising individual and small business clients on a range of tax issues, as well as personal and business matters. He has written articles for numerous publications and lectured before a wide variety of professional organizations. He was a contributing author to *How to Beat the System* (Rodale, 1997).

Allison Noel is a freelance writer who specializes in parent–child communications. She is now applying that expertise personally for the first time. She lives with her husband, Jay, in Salem, Massachusetts.

Aldo Pascarella is an award-winning screenwriter, with film projects in development at SABAN Entertainment and Brad Krevoy's newly formed production company. A graduate of Dartmouth College and the University of Southern California's Cinema–Television School, he lives in New York City.

Roni Beth Tower is a clinical psychologist with a doctorate from Yale University, specializing in issues of work and relationships. A fellow of the Academy of Clinical Psychology and past president of the American Association for the Study of Mental Imagery, she counsels adolescents, adults, and couples at her Westport, Connecticut, practice.

The Magic of Lifescripts

I've been giving advice to people for most of my adult life. Usually it's in my capacity as an attorney and financial advisor; but other times it's as a son, husband, father, or friend. Most often I'm being asked for help with vital legal and financial matters; but sometimes I'm asked how to persuade a husband to lose weight or how to borrow money from a parent.

I suppose I've become a source of advice on these diverse areas because of my long and varied experience in the law and business, my reputation as an effective negotiator, my notoriety as an author and television commentator, and the uniquely personal brand of service and attention I offer clients, readers, and viewers.

I like to take people by the hand and lead them through a process, helping them plan and preparing them for potential obstacles. I try to break every project down into manageable steps. However, despite my best efforts and explaining and coaching there's always one last question: "But what do I *say*?" It doesn't matter if I'm helping a young couple buy their first home, an experienced corporate executive negotiate an employment contract, or my father complain to his insurance company. People always want to know what words they should use and how they should deal with possible responses.

To ease their anxiety, I tell the person to telephone me before the event so we can create a "lifescript" for the whole conversation—an outline of the entire conversation including counters, responses, and rejoinders. Usually the lifescript is used verbatim, but sometimes it simply serves as the extra measure of confidence the person needs to face a difficult, unpleasant, or awkward situation. Many of my clients are amazed at how effective these lifescripts can be and how much better they fare using them.

I'd like to take total credit for the incredible efficacy of my lifescripts, but while my negotiating savvy and experiences do play a part, what really makes them work is that they're comprehensive plans for situations we usually don't plan for.

When Generals Powell and Schwarzkoff were ordered to attack the Iraqi forces occupying Kuwait, they didn't just wing it. They and their staffs sat down and planned for every eventuality. By the time they launched Operation Desert Storm, there was nothing that could surprise them. From the first moment to the last they were in charge, dictating the action. They were proactive, not reactive. Saddam Hussein and the Republican Guards didn't know what hit them.

Don't get me wrong. I'm not implying that life is a war—though we all have to deal with our share of petty tyrants and despots. What I'm saying is that if we plan out our interpersonal exchanges—whether they involve work, business, or our family lives—not only will they be easier to deal with but, more often than not, they'll turn out the way we want. With a lifescript, either directly in front of you or just in your head, you'll never be surprised. You'll have a plan that leads inexorably to your goal, regardless of what obstacle is thrown in your way. You'll have an answer to every question, a comeback to every crack, and a defense for every attack.

HOW TO USE LIFESCRIPTS

The following pages offer solutions for what are arguably thirty-eight of the most perplexing and problematic dialogues a manager will ever face.

Each lifescript begins with a general discussion of the overall *strategy* you should use in the dialogue, usually highlighting what your goal should be. Then the text briefly describes the *attitude* you should adopt, e.g. righteous indignation or contrition. The entry then touches on what kinds of *preparation* you need before using the script. This can include some research or the drafting of a memo. Next, are tips on *timing*, for instance whether it's better to have this conversation Monday morning or Friday afternoon. Then, the text explains what your *behavior* should be like. This could involve body language or where you hold the conversation.

On the next page is the lifescript itself in flow-chart form. Most offer icebreakers, pitches, possible responses, counters, and retorts. Obviously, each lifescript is different because each conversation takes a different form.

After the flow chart some ideas for *adaptations* are offered—other situations where, with some minor modifications, you could use the same lifescript. Finally, they provide a few   for each lifescript that is listed. You can use these as crib notes to bring with you to the dialogue.

These lifescripts can be used verbatim. The words have been chosen very carefully. However, I think it's best if you take the words offered and play around with them until they sound like your own. That's because everyone has different diction and sentence structure. There's nothing wrong with sounding prepared. . . as long as you sound like yourself.

With thirty-eight scripts and possible adaptations more than doubling that number, I think this book offers help in nearly every common management situation. However, I'm sure there are important situations I've left out either because the authors and I simply didn't think of them, or because they're unique to you and the circumstances of your life.

Rather than require you to call me on the telephone to help you prepare a personal script, I thought I'd give you a brief course in the five rules behind these lifescripts. That way you'll be able to draft your own. (Although, of course, you are welcome to call me if you get in a real pickle.) These are, in fact, the same rules the authors of these lifescripts followed.

Rule #1: Take Control of the Situation

If you gain nothing else from this book, let it be an understanding of this rule. The single most important element in getting these conversations to turn out the way you want is to take control of them. That doesn't mean you monopolize conversation or bully the other person. It simply means that, through your choice of words and reactions, you frame and steer it in the direction you want.

In many cases, that means you make the first move, and, by so doing, force the other person to respond. In other situations, it means responding in such a way that the other person is forced into retorts that you're already prepared to address. Unlike most *ice breakers*, these aren't written just to make the person delivering them more comfortable. They're written to force the other party into a position with a limited number of options. That way we can prepare responses to each of those limited options.

Rule #2: Say What You Want

I'm continually amazed at the inability of most people to come out and say exactly what they want. Whether it's because we don't want to be viewed as demanding or we're afraid of being turned down, most of us beat around the bush, imply, and drop hints rather than coming right out and saying what's on our mind.

In almost every lifescript there's a *pitch*, a direct specific request. You can't rely on other people to infer what you're after or to pick up on your hints. Besides, if you don't come right out and ask directly, you're giving the other party a chance to sidestep the whole issue. Make him respond directly. It's easier to deal with an outright rejection than you might imagine.

Rule #3: Show Your Power Before You Use It

Subtle demonstrations of power are often just as effective as the outright use of that power. For instance, if you're a restaurant patron you have two powers: your ability to make a scene and your willingness to pay your bill. By calling over a waiter or maitre'd and whispering that you're unhappy with your meal and would like another, you demonstrate that you're aware of your power to make a scene, but are holding it in check until they've had a chance to respond. If you actually raise your voice and make a scene immediately you have far less power because you've used up all your ammunition.

Other ways of displaying your power include saying things like, "I'm a long–time customer and would like to continue our relationship," or "The last thing I want to do is hire someone else to finish this project." In both cases you're showing an awareness of your power but a willingness not to use it. That's far more likely to work than an outright threat. Although if push comes to shove, you may have to make such a threat.

Rule #4: Absorb or Deflect Anger

That doesn't mean you should get angry, however. Displays of anger are just as self-defeating as gratuitous exercises of power. The actual message you send when you get angry is "I've no real power so all I can do is make noise." Therefore, hold your temper whenever possible.

Similarly, when you're met with anger, the best response is to disarm the other party by either absorbing or deflecting it. You absorb anger by acknowledging it and refusing to respond in kind. ("I can understand your being angry. I would be, too.") You deflect anger by suggesting that it's an odd reaction and must therefore be based on something other than your request. ("I don't understand why you're getting angry at me? Have I done something else to bother you?")

Rule #5: Have the Last Word

In almost every situation, it's to your advantage to have the last word in a dialogue. That means either expressing thanks for getting what you wanted, asking for reconsideration of a rejection, pushing for another meeting, or saying that you'll call back if you couldn't get a definite answer. Having the last word does two things: It makes sure you retain the control over the dialogue that you seized when you broke the ice and it enables you to close the conversation on advantageous terms.

The only exceptions to having the last word are in situations where it's important for you to give the other party a chance to save face. In effect, by giving him the last word, you're letting him think he's still in control, even though he's not.

TWO PHILOSOPHICAL THOUGHTS

Before you jump into the lifescripts themselves, I need to touch on two important philosophical issues: the ethics of scripting conversations in advance and the question of whether or not you use white lies to your advantage.

Some of the people I've helped develop lifescripts have voiced concerns about the ethics of scripting some dialogues. They feel workplace communication is more honest when it's spontaneous. Personally, I don't see anything wrong with preparing for office discussions, even informal ones. In fact, I think it's an excellent idea.

Sure, one of the major reasons people like my lifescripts is that they work. By using them, my clients have been able to get what they want out of life. However, that's not the only advantage to lifescripts. When you plan a conversation out to this extent, you avoid a lot of the ancillary problems of human interaction. By scripting, you avoid getting sidetracked into a discussion of why you didn't attend an employee's wedding or why no one from your department participated in the Labor Day walkathon. Granted, those may be two valid topics for discussion. However, they should be topics in and of themselves, not background noise in a dialogue about office gossiping or potential vendor problems. By scripting, you insure that the conversation will stay on track and, in the process, avoid falling into argumentative patterns. I think that, far from being unfair or unethical, lifescripts help pave the way for smoother workplace relations and better office communications.

Finally, let's look at the issue of white lies. In a few of the lifescripts, you'll notice lines such as, "I've already notified the staff about this," which effectively disarm threats from the other party. The authors are assuming that you're actually going to do what the lifescript says, in this case, speak to the staff before the meeting. Of course, that doesn't mean you have to in order to use the line. That's something you'll have to decide for yourself. But, if I can offer one more word of advice in parting, the most effective lifescripts are truthful.

Stephen M. Pollan

I

Lifescripts

...for Subordinates

Giving a Negative Performance Review

1.

STRATEGY

Delivering criticism requires a delicate touch. You need to present the problem strongly enough so the employee gets the message and hopefully changes his behavior, but not so strongly that you undermine his confidence or create lingering resentment. The best way to accomplish this is to start with positive comments before delivering the criticism. If the information is received openly, reaffirm your confidence and set up a future meeting. If the employee disputes your perception or gets angry, give him a chance to get over reflexive defensiveness by offering specifics. If that doesn't calm him down, stop pulling your punches and make it clear his future depends on improved performance.

TACTICS

- **Attitude:** Think of yourself as a teacher or mentor, not a judge and jury. Be willing to absorb a little anger without retaliating—it's not easy to take criticism submissively.
- **Preparation:** Make sure your list of criticisms is accurate and detailed— you don't want this to turn into a debate over facts. Have specific suggestions and advice ready to help the employee improve his performance.
- **Timing:** If this isn't a formal review, it should take place as soon after a problem as possible so it's fresh in everyone's mind. If you can, schedule it for early in the week so the employee has a chance to act on your advice right away and won't have to dwell on it over a weekend.
- **Behavior:** Lead off with positive comments so the meeting doesn't seem like a one-sided attack. If the employee won't get past his initial anger or denial, forget subtlety and make it clear his future is at stake unless he cleans up his act.

1. Giving a Negative Performance Review

Icebreaker: I'm generally very pleased with your work—especially the way you're handling the arrangements for the sales conference—but there is one thing you need to work on. Maybe I haven't made it clear that you're also responsible for supervising all the promotional materials, because lately I've found quite a few mistakes and some sloppy work.

Gets angry: *I've been working overtime to get everything set for the sales conference. I can't believe you're complaining about this given all I've accomplished here.*

Denies problem: *Really? I've been very careful about reviewing those pieces. I don't think there were any mistakes when they left my desk.*

Accepts criticism: *I'm really sorry. I didn't realize that I'd slipped up. I won't let it happen again.*

Chance to diffuse anger: I'm surprised by your reaction. I thought you'd be eager to improve your performance. Is there something else troubling you?

Gets over anger: *I'm sorry that I got so defensive and snapped at you. It's just that I work very hard and really want to do the best job that I can.*

Remains angry: *I think you're being very unfair. On the whole, my work has been excellent; you're just nitpicking. You've been overly critical of me from day one.*

Chance to get past denial: Let me show you what I mean. Here are copies of the last three promotional pieces that you okayed. I've marked the problem areas.

Still denies problem: *I'm not the only one whose job it is to check the promos. I can't believe that some of those mistakes weren't inserted after I signed off.*

Gets past denial: *I guess you're right. I didn't realize that all the time I was spending on the conference was affecting my other work. I'll be more careful from now on.*

Issue a warning: I have a real problem with your uncooperative attitude. If you want to make it in this company, you'll need to address this problem. Please come back to me in a day or so to discuss how you propose to handle it.

Schedule a meeting: I'm so glad to hear you say that and I want to help you in any way I can. Let's schedule a meeting for a month from now to talk about how things are progressing.

ADAPTATIONS

This script can be modified to:
- Review a student's poor performance.
- Discuss a partner's lack of effort.
- Speak with a volunteer about lethargic efforts.

KEY POINTS

- Soften initial criticism by suggesting that perhaps your instructions weren't clear or that the employee has been overworked.
- If your criticism is denied, offer specifics without getting defensive.
- If the employee responds with anger, show surprise and ask if there's something else troubling him.
- If the employee accepts the criticism immediately, or after having a chance to blow off some steam, reiterate your desire to help and schedule a subsequent meeting.
- If the employee refuses to get past his anger or denial, say you have a problem with his attitude, warn him it must change, and demand immediate action.

Turning Down a Subordinate's Raise Request

STRATEGY

In many situations it's easy to turn down a raise request: A performance not up to expectations is a justifiable reason to maintain a salary level. If a person bases her request on what others are making, it's easy to explain that everyone is treated as an individual. The difficult dialogue is when you have to deny a request from someone who, in fact, merits an increase, but who can't get one because of the company's financial situation. The secret here is to hammer home the fact that she is a valued employee who is making a legitimate request that simply can't be met right now because of the company's financial situation. Every rational person realizes you can't get water from a stone. Temper her justifiable disappointment by stressing that you will come back to her with a raise, based on her presentation, as soon as the financial picture brightens.

TACTICS

- **Attitude:** Accept that in tough economic times the needs of the company must come first. Simply maintaining staff is often a sacrifice for struggling companies.
- **Preparation:** You'll have little opportunity to prepare unless you're given advance warning of what the meeting will be about. In that unlikely case, documentation of the company's financial problems could help ease the pain.
- **Timing:** You'll have little or no control over when this meeting takes place because it will be instigated by the employee. After asked, don't delay or stall.
- **Behavior:** Be compassionate, caring, and understanding. There's no need to apologize, however. It's just a fact of life that when a company's business is off its employees will have to forego raises.

2. Turning Down a Subordinate's Raise Request

Icebreaker: *I need to thank you for the opportunity you and the company have given me. I recognize that you've been very influential in my growth and advancement. However, I have a problem that I need your help with.*

Show concern: I think you know that I'm always here if you need my help. What's the problem and what can I do?

Professional growth:
What has happened is that I've been concentrating solely on my professional growth and haven't been paying any attention to my stream of income. I've done some research and found my peers are earning on average 15 percent more than my current compensation. I've drafted this memo. It's logical for my compensation to keep pace with my growth. To do that I'll need an increase of . . .

Contribution up: *I think my salary no longer reflects my contribution to the company. In the past year I've helped the company save a great deal of money [or] bring in added revenue [or] trim quite a bit from the cost of operations. I've done some research and I've found that a salary of . . . would more accurately reflect my value. I've prepared a brief memo outlining my accomplishments and my request.*

Responsibilities up: *I think my salary no longer matches my job responsibilities. During the past year I've moved from being an order taker to helping supervise the evening staff and helping draft the new sales scripts. I've done some research and I think a salary of . . . would more accurately reflect my responsibilities. I've prepared a brief memo outlining my increased responsibilities and my request.*

Anniversary raise: *I've come to ask you for a raise of 10 percent. It's been a year since my last increase and in the past the company has had a policy of giving annual raises on the anniversary of our coming aboard.*

Universal response: Although you may not be aware of it, I've been watching you carefully and have tried to help nurture your development. The company would never consciously be unfair to you, and neither would I. The company has always done its level best, consistent with its obligations to the stockholders [or] owners. I want you to know that we love having you here. I'm aware of everything that you've said [or] I'm sure your memo makes your case persuasively, however, there's no budget for a raise for you right now. You do have an excellent future with this company if you continue on this track, and we do appreciate all you've been doing.

Not a partner: *I understand what you're saying. You're asking me to participate in the success or failure of the company, but I'm not an owner [or] a partner.*

That's no help: *I'm glad to hear you say I have a future here, but my stream of income is important to me. While I'm flattered, your praise doesn't help me pay my daughter's college tuition.*

No commitment: *Are you saying you can't give me any kind of commitment about a raise in the near future?*

You and company linked: That's where you're wrong. To the extent the company succeeds financially you will as well. And, unfortunately, to the extent the company must sacrifice financially, you will have to also.

Personal commitment: I personally will give you a commitment that when things improve, I will come to you with an increase, based on the presentation you made today. You won't have to come back to me again.

ADAPTATIONS

This script can be modified to:

- Deny requests for non-monetary benefits that could create morale problems.

KEY POINTS

- Let the employee make her pitch without interruption or argument.
- If correct, accept her assertions and numbers openly.
- Respond to every request, regardless of which pitch is used, with the same answer: The money isn't there right now.
- Accept a certain amount of anger, sullenness, or annoyance—it's understandable.
- Make a personal commitment to come back with an increase as soon as it's possible.

Adding Responsibility to a Subordinate without More Pay

3.

STRATEGY

It's a fact of life today. Almost every manager will one day need to ask a subordinate to take on more work without being able to offer him any more pay in compensation. The secret to making this a smooth discussion is to frame it as good news. Don't feel manipulative. Because the alternative is unemployment, it is good news. Astute employees will realize that and go along with your spin...at least superficially. Feel free to point out that the added responsibilities will increase their value and marketability. Employees who aren't as swift or who take a piece–work attitude toward their jobs will need to have it made crystal clear to them that if they want to keep their jobs they'll do what they're told. If they're not willing to accept that, they are free to look elsewhere.

TACTICS

- **Attitude:** Realize that this really is good news. You could be telling this person he is terminated. Instead, you're telling him he still has a job.
- **Preparation:** Give some thought to the employee's attitude toward his job. That will make his response less of a surprise.
- **Timing:** As soon as you're made aware of the new arrangements, tell your subordinates. You don't want them to hear it from the grapevine. If it comes from you first, you'll be able to put things in perspective.
- **Behavior:** Don't be gleeful about the situation, but on the other hand, there's no need to be glum either. This is a fact of life in today's workplace, so treat it as such.

3. Adding Responsibility to a Subordinate without More Pay

Icebreaker and pitch: I have some good news so I came right over to tell you. Your job is safe now. I was able to convince the people upstairs that our department could cut costs by becoming more efficient, rather than by downsizing. They've decided to cut a position in international sales instead and pass some work on to us.

Work load objection: *Does that mean we're going to have to start staying later? [or] I'm already overloaded, I guess I won't be able to take those night classes.*

Little price to pay: Yes, I suppose so, but that's a small price to pay for holding onto our jobs in this kind of economy. Don't you agree?

Financial objection: *I hope I'll be getting a pay raise to go along with the increase in my responsibilities and the change in my job description.*

Look long term: No, I'm afraid not. But look at the long–term benefit. It's an opportunity to prove ourselves, increase our skills, and improve our job profiles. All of that will help in the future–either here or someplace else.

Piece–work attitude: *Still, I expect to be paid for the work I do. If I do more, I expect to be paid more.*

Grudging acceptance: *I suppose you're right . . . but I'm used to getting paid for the work I do.*

The company needs us: I understand. It's perfectly reasonable to want to be adequately compensated. But right now we're going to have to put that aside and help the company pull through this crisis period.

Evaluate your job: I understand. If you feel that strongly, perhaps you need to evaluate how important this job is to you . . . if in fact it is.

ADAPTATIONS

This script can be modified to:

- Give more tasks to a day worker without increasing his hours.
- Get a contractor to increase the scope of his work without increasing his bid.

KEY POINTS

- Present this as good news.
- If the employee objects to the increased work load, point out he could have no work.
- If the employee objects on financial grounds, explain that in the long run, the added responsibilities will increase his value . . . either here or somewhere else.
- If the employee still balks and is a valuable member of your team, say this is something he will simply have to accept for the good of the company.
- If the employee still balks and isn't a key person, say he can leave if he doesn't like it.

Announcing a Salary Reduction to a Subordinate

4

STRATEGY

Here's one of the more difficult workplace dialogues in this book. Reducing salary is a tough thing to do. There's bound to be a great deal of anger on the part of the employee so don't be glib or try to put too positive a spin on the situation. The great danger here is that the employee will take it as a sign she isn't appreciated and will look elsewhere for a job. That's why it's essential you do everything you can to impress on her that you'd like to keep her. At the same time you can't pull any punches. Don't imply it's only temporary if you know it's intended to be permanent, and don't promise to make it up to her in other areas if you can't. One secret is to go to the employee's office rather than having her come to yours. That reduces some of the fear and also puts you more in the role of supplicant. Normally, that's not appropriate, but in this case you are a supplicant. You're asking her to stick around even though you're cutting her pay.

TACTICS

- **Attitude:** Accept that you're asking the employee to give up a great deal and that a bit of fear and anger on her part is justifiable.
- **Preparation:** Make sure you understand the organization's rationale for the pay cut and can explain it succinctly. It's essential you use the same explanation with every person you speak with. Mixed messages will imply a hidden agenda and that will destroy the already battered morale.
- **Timing:** Present the news as soon as you know it's official, regardless of the time of day, day of week, or status of any other activities. This may require dramatic action on the part of employees and they deserve as much lead time as you can give them.
- **Behavior:** Do all that you can to reassure the employee that her job is safe and her future with the company secure. Absorb anger—it's a legitimate response to these circumstances. Be as compassionate as you can, but refrain from making promises you can't keep or sugarcoating the news.

15

4. Announcing a Salary Reduction to a Subordinate

Icebreaker and pitch: I wanted to speak with you for a few minutes about how the company is changing in response to increased competition, that's why I'm here. The company is very concerned with your long-term happiness. In fact, that's why I'm here. The last thing we want to do is cut staff, especially productive team players like you. But our recent round of management audits pointed out that we need to reduce our payroll. That's why starting next month there will be an across-the-board salary reduction of 5 percent.

Fearful: *Please be honest with me. Are you really telling me I should look for another job?*

Offer reassurance: On the contrary, we look at you as a partner in this. We want to keep you on board. If we wanted to get rid of you, we would have. It's our goal to keep all of our valued employees—and you are someone we value very highly.

Is it temporary?: *I assume this is a temporary reduction. When will we all be brought back up to our normal salaries?*

Stress permanence: This isn't a temporary reaction to a problem, it's a permanent restructuring. In effect, we're creating a brand new company to meet the challenges of the coming years.

Self-centered: *But I've helped increase revenues by more than 10 percent in the past year. You told me how well I'd done at my last review. Is this how the company rewards achievement?*

Not criticism: This has nothing to do with your performance. The cuts are being made to keep the company alive and healthy. And whatever is in the long-term good of the company helps you as well.

Quid pro quo: *What is the company offering in exchange for all that I'm losing with this reduction?*

Can't afford it: *I can't afford a salary reduction. In fact, based on my positive review, I was planning on asking you for an increase soon.*

Issues threat: *I hope you understand that this means I'm going to have to start looking for another job.*

Be frank: Frankly, we're offering you employment with a healthy company that is positioned well for the coming years and that has an extraordinary future ahead of it.

Show concern: The company wants you to stay. I want you to stay. I care about you and your family. You have a very promising future here if you choose to remain a part of our team. I hope you will.

Offer sympathy: I'm not surprised to hear that. I know that I may cause some short-term problems for you and your budget. We're all going to have to tighten our belts. All I can offer you is a wonderful long-term future in exchange for the short-term discomfort.

ADAPTATIONS

This script can be modified to:
- Reduce staff, benefits, or perquisites.
- Increase employee's contribution toward medical or pension plan.
- Transfer an employee.

KEY POINTS

- Be clear and direct, presenting this as an unavoidable and final decision that doesn't reflect on the employee's performance or standing in the organization.
- If the employee cites her own success in response, reiterate that the cut isn't linked to performance, it's across the board based on the company's needs.
- If the employee asks if it's temporary or asks what she'll be receiving in exchange, be honest.
- If the employee expresses fears about her position, reassure her that this isn't a question of performance.
- If the employee expresses fears about her finances, commiserate but stress that there's no alternative.
- If the employee asks if you're taking a reduction, be truthful.
- If the employee threatens to look for another job, stress the company's desire to retain her, but accept that there's nothing you can do to stop her.

Telling a Subordinate to Watch His Drinking

5.

STRATEGY

In large organizations, there are official policies for dealing with employee drug and alcohol problems and, perhaps, on-staff individuals trained in bringing up such issues with employees. But most small companies have no formal procedures or resources for these troubling matters. Instead, it often falls to a manager. If you're eager to retain the individual, you're going to need to impress on him the need to rehabilitate or, at the very least, to clean up his act during working hours. Expect anger, denial, and projection, but reiterate that this is a workplace problem that needs to be addressed. Regardless of how the dialogue ends, offer whatever information about treatment you can and then keep your fingers crossed that the shock therapy works.

TACTICS

- **Attitude:** Be determined. Employees' personal problems cannot be allowed to interfere with the workings of the company. An employee with a drinking problem is a danger to both you and the company.
- **Preparation:** Find out all you can about the company's health insurance coverage for such problems as well as local programs or facilities.
- **Timing:** Do this as soon as possible after an incident in which the employee's problem was obvious.
- **Behavior:** Hold this meeting in your office. Make sure it's entirely private and confidential. Be as businesslike as possible. It's not your role to explore the causes of the problem—leave that to a counselor. Stress that you're talking about the shortcomings of his performance on the job, not his personal behavior. Your goal is to make it clear that his behavior is affecting his work and that you cannot allow that to continue.

5. Telling a Subordinate to Watch His Drinking

Icebreaker: I called you in here to tell you that your job performance is not as good as it should be, and that I think the reason is your drinking during business hours.

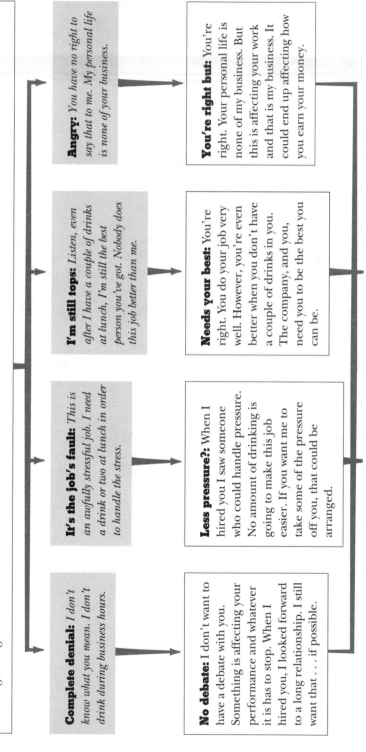

Complete denial: *I don't know what you mean. I don't drink during business hours.*

It's the job's fault: *This is an awfully stressful job. I need a drink or two at lunch in order to handle the stress.*

I'm still tops: *Listen, even after I have a couple of drinks at lunch, I'm still the best person you've got. Nobody does this job better than me.*

Angry: *You have no right to say that to me. My personal life is none of your business.*

No debate: I don't want to have a debate with you. Something is affecting your performance and whatever it is has to stop. When I hired you, I looked forward to a long relationship. I still want that . . . if possible.

Less pressure?: When I hired you I saw someone who could handle pressure. No amount of drinking is going to make this job easier. If you want me to take some of the pressure off you, that could be arranged.

Needs your best: You're right. You do your job very well. However, you're even better when you don't have a couple of drinks in you. The company, and you, need you to be the best you can be.

You're right but: You're right. Your personal life is none of my business. But this is affecting your work and that is my business. It could end up affecting how you earn your money.

Apologizes: *I'm sorry. I'll handle it. It won't happen again.*

Confrontational: *Are you threatening me?*

Accept apology: Thanks. I was hoping you'd respond that way. I know you care about this company and want to do the best job you can. If I can be of any help, let me know.

I don't want to: We're having this conversation because I don't want to have to fire you. I'll fire you only if I have no other choice. We have a problem here. I need you to address it. I'll help if I can, but it has to be addressed.

Provide information: I've checked and the company's health insurance plan will cover outpatient treatment and counseling. Here's a list of services and practitioners in the area.

ADAPTATIONS

This script can be modified to:
- Stop an employee from proselytizing in the office.
- Stop an employee from gossiping.
- Curtail disruptive behavioral problems, such as loud radios.

KEY POINTS

- Be businesslike, determined, clear, and direct. Remember this is a business discussion even though it revolves around a personal problem.
- If the employee denies he has a problem, refuse to get into a debate. Indeed, stress that there's a problem that must be corrected.
- If the employee blames job–related stress for his drinking, offer to help relieve some stress.
- If the employee claims his performance is still good despite his drinking, say that it could be better yet.
- If the employee says it's personal, agree, but note that when personal problems affect the workplace they become business problems.
- If the employee remains confrontational, say his job is in jeopardy.

Turning down a Subordinate's Promotion Request

6

STRATEGY

Despite the changes in the workplace, most employees believe that positions should be filled from within by moving individuals up the chain of command. Today, however, such strict adherence to hierarchy isn't the norm. Openings are usually filled on a case–by–case basis, or not at all. Sometimes people are moved laterally; sometimes a replacement is brought in from outside; and sometimes people are indeed moved up the ladder. When an employee requests a promotion you cannot grant, the secret to breaking the bad news is to offer her praise and explain that her future lies elsewhere, to say she isn't quite ready for the job, or to suggest that the particular job description will be changed, making her experience—her major selling point—irrelevant. All three must be done gently, particularly if the person has a promising future in the company. Keep this discussion short and sweet. You're breaking the news of the decision, not engaging in another job interview. If the employee doesn't accept your primary rationale, be friendly but firm and note that she isn't the one who makes these decisions.

TACTICS

- **Attitude:** Think of yourself as a coach, inspiring a player to try again after falling short.
- **Preparation:** Decide prior to the meeting how important the employee will be to the company's future. If she does figure strongly in your plans, discuss these, vaguely, reassuring her of her value. If she's not likely to play an important role in the company's future, you can lean more toward her not being ready for the job.
- **Timing:** Do this as soon as you know she won't be getting the job. The last thing you want is for her to hear it through the grapevine before you've had a chance to add your spin to the message.
- **Behavior:** Be concise and businesslike. You're not passing a death sentence. Offer your best explanation and then move on, refusing to engage in another job interview.

6. Turning down a Subordinate's Promotion Request

Icebreaker: Joan, I've called you in here to let you know that you won't be taking Jack's place as manager of the department. I have other plans for you. I want to thank you for making yourself available for the job. Once again you've demonstrated how much you care for the company's success and we're excited about your future here.

Why not?: *I don't understand why I'm not getting Jack's job. I replaced him when he was on vacation. I'm the next in line. I've covered for him when he was sick. I know everything he does. Even he said I was the best person for the job.*

What plans?: *Naturally I'm disappointed, but I'm excited to hear you and the company have plans for me. If they're not for me to take Jack's place, what are they?*

Job changed: The job Jack did may no longer exist. We're reviewing the structure of the entire department and, in all likelihood, there will no longer be a manager's position. However, let me repeat that we admire your sense of urgency and your ambition, and there is a future for you here.

Not ready: You're not ready yet. Moving you into this kind of spot prematurely would do more harm than good to your long-term future. When you're more seasoned, you may well be moved into a more important position. Let me repeat, there's a future for you here—we just don't want to see you self-destruct.

No specifics: Actually, we believe your progress in the company may not follow the traditional path. There's nothing specific just yet, but we're considering you in our long-term plans. You're part of a group that we'd like to play a major role in our future.

Hidden agenda?: *You make being turned down sound wonderful, but I've still been turned down. Is there some other agenda? Are you sending me a message about my career here?*

Close the issue: Listen. We're happy with you. We want you to stay with us. I've said we think you're valuable and you have a future here. [Smile] However, we're not about to have you tell us how to run the company. You may get to that position one day . . . but you're not there yet.

ADAPTATIONS

This script can be modified to:
- Turn down a transfer request.
- Turn down a request for a change of title.

KEY POINTS

- Be clear, direct, and concise, holding out the suggestion of a future with the company.
- Let her ask for a reason because she may instead ask about your suggestion of an alternative future for her, getting you into a more positive line of conversation.
- If she does ask for a reason, say she's not ready or the job will be changed.
- If she asks about her future, remain vague but hopeful.
- If she tries to engage in a further dialogue, cut her short, wielding your authority firmly but with good humor.

Reprimanding an Alleged Sexual Harasser

7

STRATEGY

Surprisingly, it's easier to confront someone who's sexually harassing you personally than someone who's accused by a third party. That's because in the first instance you're certain of the facts and can have a one-on-one, person-to-person dialogue that transcends office hierarchy. On the other hand, when one subordinate complains to you about the actions of another, you can never be certain of the facts and must be just as concerned about the rights of the accused as the rights of the accuser. That being said, it's vital you make some kind of prejudgment—based on either careful questioning of the accuser or prior experience with the accused—about whether or not you believe the conduct in question was intentionally harassing. Treat an unintended harasser harshly and you could be needlessly hurtful and jeopardize his future performance. Treat a malevolent harasser gently and you risk not stopping the behavior and incurring legal liability. Your judgment will probably be made clear by the accused's response to the situation. Whatever develops, the secret in this script is to focus attention, not on the actions or intent of the accused, but on the perceptions of the accuser.

TACTICS

- **Attitude:** Your goal is to make sure such a problem never happens again, so the facts of the situation aren't as important as putting your foot down . . . firmly.
- **Preparation:** Question the accuser closely and consider the past record and actions of the accused. Then come up with a prejudgment on whether you believe the actions were intentionally harassing.
- **Timing:** Do this as soon as possible after the incident in question. Make sure to hold the conversation during business hours so the accused knows this is a business, not personal, issue.
- **Behavior:** Hold this meeting in your office. Make sure it's just as private and confidential as your meeting with the accuser. Be as businesslike as possible. It's not your role to determine the facts of the case. It's your job to make sure it doesn't happen again.

7. Reprimanding an Alleged Sexual Harasser

Icebreaker: Jane has told me about your conduct. She regards it as harassment.

Believe malevolent: This is an extremely serious problem that threatens you and your career as well as the company. We must nip this problem in the bud.

Believe unintentional: This is an extremely serious problem for the company, regardless of what you had in mind. We must nip this problem in the bud.

Can't understand: *I can't imagine what I could have said or done that would make her feel I was harassing her. I feel terrible.*

Doesn't matter: In a situation like this, your intent doesn't matter. All that matters is her perception of your words or actions. We have to address her complaint promptly.

Denies behavior: *Listen, I don't know what she's talking about. I didn't do or say anything to her that was in the least bit sexual.*

Blames victim: *Hey, you know what she's like. She's got no sense of humor. She's a real prude. I was just joking around.*

He has problem: I don't know if Jane has a problem or not. But you clearly have a problem now. You've got to take care of this situation.

Perception is issue: What you did or didn't do isn't the issue here. What matters is her perception. You've got to take care of this situation.

Forceful pitch: You are not to have any personal interaction with Jane and are to keep your business interaction with her to the absolute minimum required to get your job done. Try to have a third party present. I will convey your apologies to her. One other thing. I don't want to have to speak to you about this kind of situation ever again.

Clueless: *What do you want me to do about it?*

Wants to help: *Please tell me what I can do to clear this up.*

Pitch solution: Just stay as far away from her as you can. I will convey your apologies to her. Don't have any personal conversations with her. If you have to talk with her about business, keep it brief and to the point. . . . and try to have a third party present. This is not a situation we want to see continue or escalate.

ADAPTATIONS

This script can be modified to:
- Question an employee about a reported possible theft.

KEY POINTS

- If you suspect intent, stress the potential impact of this charge on the accused's career. Otherwise, stress the potential harm to the company.
- If he denies doing anything wrong, say his actions aren't the issue, her perceptions are.
- If he blames the victim, say she isn't in trouble, he is.
- If he doesn't seem to catch on to his problem, forcefully suggest a solution.
- If he seems eager to make amends, suggest a solution.

Stopping Backstabbing among Subordinates 8.

STRATEGY

If the coffee break is the number one entitlement workers hold sacred, complaining is a close second. Employees consider gripe sessions as no more than a healthy "venting" of petty frustrations. But when someone repeatedly and maliciously directs complaints at colleagues behind their backs, it's not only the employee that's being attacked but also the efficiency of the work place. The goal of this script is to bring such backstabbing to an immediate halt. The secret is investigation and verification. If you haven't witnessed the backstabbing first hand, you must verify it. That's because it's not uncommon for an employee to try to manipulate management into punishing an office enemy by alleging backstabbing. Verifying a complaint means interviewing all the affected workers, including the alleged perpetrator. Quite often the investigation is enough to bring the problem to a halt: Word spreads you're aware of the problem, consider it serious, and are ready to deal with it accordingly.

TACTICS

- **Attitude:** Everything you do or say must demonstrate that management considers backstabbing a serious offense. Remember, as a manager you must overcome the time-worn "venting" viewpoint as well as the silent discomfort inherent in investigating employee–versus–employee issues. To do that your attitude must be serious and straightforward every step of the way.
- **Preparation:** The unease workers feel bringing backstabbing to the attention of management is part of the shield protecting the abusive subordinate. You must be prepared to penetrate this wall of silence. Subordinates should be told they're not being singled out but are among many being interviewed. Emphasize that all responses are strictly confidential. Solicit feedback about the problem in general without attaching a name to initial queries. However, once initiated, the interview should call upon specific incidents, and you must press for the identification of a specific individual. Collective anonymity can provide a cover that encourages honest responses. It will also add considerable weight to the meeting with the actual backstabber.

8. Stopping Backstabbing among Subordinates

Establish control: Jan, we have a serious problem. One of our staff is constantly criticizing and demeaning the work of others behind their backs. It's at the point where morale and productivity are going downhill. Such backstabbing is very upsetting. After personal observation [or] a thorough investigation, I've no doubt you're the person responsible for the turmoil.

Confirms role: *I complain like everyone else. I never meant any harm.*

Deflects accusation: *I don't believe this! Everyone complains. I do my job every day, no problem. Why are you singling me out?*

Validates accusation: You've singled yourself out. You know I carefully investigated this problem. You were one of the many people I interviewed. A number of your coworkers—a number, not just one—made it clear you are the source of the problem.

Makes excuses: *This is unfair. I don't care what any of them said. They don't like me because I don't socialize with them. I don't believe you'd let them do this to me.*

Re-asserts authority: It's too late for excuses. I wouldn't accuse you or anyone else of anything if I hadn't taken the time to make sure I was right. If you think this is unfair, you can go over my head. We can both put our cases on the table. Just give me the word.

Establish conditions: Your comments went far beyond complaining. It stops right here, right now. Any further incidents and your job is in jeopardy.

Accepts conditions: *I understand. As I said, I didn't mean to hurt anyone. I was just joking around. I'm sorry. It won't happen again.*

Wants to appeal: *Fine. Please set it up as quickly as possible.*

Rationalized acceptance: *That won't be necessary. I was just blowing off steam. Maybe I got carried away. I didn't mean to hurt anyone, I was just joking around.*

Present expectation: Your actions were far from funny. You've placed your job in jeopardy and severely strained your relationship with your coworkers. Your "joking" will stop immediately. Any such incidents in the future will cost you your job.

- **Timing:** Move quickly in confronting the problem. This shows the seriousness of the issue and the depth of your resolve in dealing with it. When you have finished gathering verification, notify the guilty employee in writing of the date and time of a meeting to discuss "a matter of serious mutual concern."
- **Behavior:** Establish that you consider the problem serious and that you're unquestionably in charge of solving it. Stay behind your desk, seated. Be straightforward and specific. Deal with the problem as an existing one, not a suspected one. Review what the problem is, how you verified it, and what you'll do about it. Don't engage in debate. Say you have the verification and want the problem to stop. Conclude the meeting by citing what specific action you will take if there are further occurrences of the problem.

ADAPTATIONS

This script can be modified to:
- Respond to other types of nonsexual harassment in the workplace.

KEY POINTS

- Take all observed or reported incidents of backstabbing very seriously.
- Verify that the behavior took place. Never act on hearsay or inconclusive evidence.
- Confront the individual involved from a position of absolute certainty—no debating.
- Be straightforward and humorless in presenting information and eliciting responses.
- Be unrelenting in underscoring the seriousness of backstabbing behavior.
- Be absolutely clear about what will happen if the behavior occurs again.

Insisting on Better Hygiene from a Subordinate

9

STRATEGY

Having to tell someone his breath or body odor is offensive may be one of the most awkward situations you'll ever face in the workplace. Yet sometimes it's essential that you take action, not only for the comfort of you and other coworkers, but for the company and the person's future as well. Such problems are almost certain to undermine the image of the company if the offending employee comes in contact with clients. Hygiene problems will erode his standing in the company and will block any future progress in the organization. Begin with the assumption that he isn't conscious of the problem. Start off by subtly suggesting the same tool(s) you use to avoid similar problems. If he takes the hint, let the matter drop. If your subtext isn't understood, you'll have to press further.

TACTICS

- **Attitude:** Try not to be embarrassed. The other party will be embarrassed enough for both of you. Remember, you're doing this for the person's own good.
- **Preparation:** Buy some breath mints or look around for a nearby drug store.
- **Timing:** Do this immediately after lunch and privately. That way you minimize embarrassment and have an excuse for your actions.
- **Behavior:** Start off being subtle, but if necessary, shift to sincere concern. There's no need to be apologetic because you're doing the person a favor.

9. Insisting on Better Hygiene from a Subordinate

Bad breath: [Show mints, pop one in your mouth.] Would you like one? I don't know about you, but sometimes I really need these after lunch.

Body odor: You won't believe the sale I stumbled on. The drug store up the street was offering 50 percent off on antiperspirants and deodorants. You should check it out. If you want, I'll go over there with you after work.

Takes the hint: *Um . . . sure. I'll take one. [or] Oh, I never . . . uh . . . Thanks, I appreciate it.*

Doesn't take hint: *No thanks. I never use those kinds of things.*

Be direct: There are some things even your best friend is too embarrassed to tell you, but you should know. You have a discernible body [or] breath odor and you need to address it. I'm bringing this up primarily for your own good because it could cause you problems.

Gets angry: *Excuse me. Are you suggesting there's something wrong with me?*

Gets defensive: *I don't have a problem—you do. No one else has said anything to me. This is just a way to humiliate me isn't it? Well, it's not going to work.*

Reasonable excuse: *I'm sorry. I've been having extensive dental work [or] I've been taking a prescription medicine and was told this might be a side effect. I'm not sure what I can do about it, however.*

You are the company: This isn't an attempt to humiliate or intimidate you. As an employee, you're a representative of the company. The impression you make reflects on it. I'm simply asking you to take care of a problem. That's all.

Embarrassed acceptance: *Oh, I'm so embarrassed. It's just that . . . I'm sorry. I'll take care of it.*

Suggest professional help: I thought it might be something like that. Why don't you give your dentist [or] pharmacist a call and ask for advice. Until then, why don't you try these [indicating breath mints or deodorant].

ADAPTATIONS

This script can be modified to:
- Discuss hygiene problems with a teen.
- Discuss hygiene problems or erratic behavior with a parent or older relative.

KEY POINTS

- Start off subtly, but if necessary, be direct.
- If he takes the hint, drop the issue.
- If he doesn't take the hint, be direct.
- If he gets angry, say it's a business problem, too.
- If he says it's none of your business, explain why it is something you need to be concerned with.

Terminating a Subordinate

10

STRATEGY

Companies have been using lay–offs as a cost–cutting strategy for years. However, even though firing employees is an all–too–common part of their duties, few managers handle the process well. That's because, whatever the facts of the dismissal, most managers feel bad about letting someone go. Ironically, expressing those feelings of remorse can be cruel because they give the employee false hope. Instead, the best way to deal with a termination is to make it a quick, unambiguous act. Spell out exactly why you are letting the employee go, state clearly that the decision is final, and explain the details of the company's severance policy. Then ask the employee to sign a letter of acknowledgment and agreement which will make it more difficult for her to reopen the discussion or sue. Resist all attempts to turn the discussion into an argument or debate. The decision has been made and it's final.

TACTICS

- **Attitude:** Whatever your feelings, be dispassionate and businesslike—it's actually in the employee's best interests.
- **Preparation:** Have documentation of poor performance if any on hand. Also have details of the severance package written into a termination letter that can be signed at this meeting. Have severance checks written out and signed prior to the meeting.
- **Timing:** Do this as early in the week and as early in the day as possible so the individual can apply for unemployment benefits and start looking for a job immediately.
- **Behavior:** Hold this meeting in your office. If possible, have a third party on hand to deter anger. Offer immediate severance payment in exchange for immediate signing of the termination memo. Absorb anger, deflect guilt, and acknowledge the employee's right to legal representation. Resist efforts to negotiate more severance or a second chance.

10. Terminating a Subordinate

Opener: I have bad news for you. I'm afraid your employment here is being terminated. The company has already cut a check for one month's severance pay and prepared a reference letter for you. I can give you both now.

Laid off for economic reasons: I'm sorry but this decision is final. It was based on the company's bottom-line profitability and has nothing to do with your performance. If asked, the company will say it was your decision to leave and I'll be happy to add my personal recommendation. If you sign this letter that outlines what I've just said, we can get this unhappy business over with.

Fired for poor performance: I must stress this decision is final. It was based on your inability to rebound from two unsatisfactory performance reviews. However, because we know you've tried, if asked, the company will say you were laid off for economic reasons. If you sign this letter that says you understand our discussion, we can put this behind us.

Defends professional record: *I have to take exception to your decision to single me out. I think I've performed as well as anyone else in the department. I've never had anyone call my skills and abilities into question before.*

Gets teary or personal: *How could you do this to me? We've been friends. I've had you over to my home for dinner. Isn't there something you can do?*

Gets angry: *I expected something like this to happen. You've had it in for me from day one. You're just using me as a scapegoat for your own mistakes.*

Absorb anger: I'm sorry you feel that way. Everyone here, especially me, wanted to see your relationship with the company work out. Unfortunately, it simply hasn't. Why don't you look at this letter and then sign it.

Deflect guilt: I feel terrible about this, but it's strictly a business decision. I can't let my personal feelings get in the way of the company's bottom line. I hope you understand. As your friend, I'll be happy to do everything I can to help you land another job. For now, though, I need you to take a look at this letter and then sign it.

Deflect defense: As I mentioned before, this is purely an economic decision having nothing to do with your abilities. You were simply the last hired. [or] We're not questioning your skills and abilities. We've simply decided that you're not as productive as we need you to be. That's something we warned you about in two prior reviews.

Demands more severance: *I'm not going to sign anything until we've had a chance to talk about this severance package. I've worked here for two years, and with the job market the way it is, this simply isn't enough.*

Threatens legal action: *I'm not going to sign anything until I speak with my attorney. I think there are some issues I need to get a legal opinion on.*

Asks for another chance: *Isn't there something I can do? I need this job. I promise my work will improve. All I need is another chance.*

Not negotiable: I'm afraid my hands are tied when it comes to the severance offer. You can speak with the chairman if you'd like, but I must tell you that she is aware of, and approved, the offer. Please sign this so I can give you your check and reference letter.

State rights: You have every right to speak with your attorney if you'd like. I'll hold onto the check and paperwork until I hear from you. [Stand up.] Good day.

Stress finality: I'm terribly sorry but the decision really is final. Please sign this so I can give you your check and reference letter.

ADAPTATIONS

This script can be modified to:
- Terminate a professional.
- Terminate an independent contractor.

KEY POINTS

- Be dispassionate, efficient, and businesslike.
- If she gets angry, absorb the outburst and push for closure.
- If she gets defensive, deflect the effort and push for closure.
- If she gets personal, deflect the guilt, stress this is business, and push for closure.
- If she gets teary, retain a businesslike demeanor, give her a chance to do the same, and then push for closure.
- Deny requests for more severance or a second chance.
- If she threatens legal action, acknowledge her right to representation.

Demanding Better Work Habits from a Subordinate

11.

STRATEGY

Time really is money. The time-shaving employee—late in, early out—is stealing from you and the company. You are paying a full-time salary for less than full-time service. The longer the problem is ignored, the more comfortable the offender feels in continuing and adding to this behavior. By dealing effectively with this one individual, you'll also help insure others don't emulate his behavior. Even though you'll be confronting the subordinate's actual behavior, expect a torrent of excuses as to why the behavior took place. Stress that *what* has happened is the issue, not *why* it has happened. Focus on what has taken place and the effect it is having on both cost and job effectiveness. Stick to this tack, and the individual will ultimately acknowledge his destructive behavior. After he does, be clear about the outcome if the abuse continues. Only then should you consider ending the meeting on a practical, humanistic note by offering advice to help the employee deal with the "whys" of his problem.

TACTICS

- **Attitude:** Be totally confident and at ease. You hold all the cards going in. You'll be citing a problem easily observed and documented. A vacant work station is a red flag. And, if there's a timeclock, you have ironclad evidence. The actual time shaving and the cost in money and job effectiveness are undeniable. Be confident and indignant that such obvious and blatant behavior is taking place.
- **Preparation:** At the point you realize there's a pattern of neglect, start writing down dates and times the employee is away from the job. Documenting these specifics is the most critical part of your preparation. Create a "memorandum for the record" indicating what you're doing and why. This becomes part of the documentation. Clearly, if the subordinate's actions hadn't prompted it, there would be no such memo. Time sheets or cards are obvious support to be gathered. Comments from other managers who have experienced similar behavior aren't necessary, but could augment your evidence.

11. Demanding Better Work Habits from a Subordinate

Establish control: [Holding up papers.] Friday, September 12th, 9:20. Tuesday, September 16th, 4:48. Wednesday, September 17th, 9:13. Friday, September 19th, 4:50. Frank, do you know what all these numbers mean?

Anxious curiosity: *No, I'm afraid I don't.*

State problem: Those are all the times you were supposed to be at your workstation but weren't. You were either not here yet or on your way home early. If you add them all up it amounts to hours of wasted work time.

Personal excuses: *I'm sorry, I've had a lot on my mind. There are things going on at home that I didn't want to burden anyone with. My head just hasn't been in the job.*

Continued focus: I can understand that, but if you're going to keep working here, you must show up and leave on time. Right now you're costing us money and effectiveness. It has got to stop.

Rationalization: *I'm not the only one. Everyone is late once in a while or cuts out early.*

Re-affirm problem: I'm aware of that. In your case, however, it's more than once in a while–otherwise I wouldn't have started keeping a record. You need to understand that your job is on the line.

Begins excuses: *I know I'm late once in a while and leave early now and then, but I didn't think it amounted to that much time.*

Confirm accusation: [Wave your papers.] You wouldn't be here if it didn't. You're costing us money and affecting your coworkers. You're also placing your job in jeopardy.

Acknowledges responsibility: *My job! I can't lose my job. I'm sorry, it won't happen any more. I swear.*

Acceptance: *I hear what you're saying. I'll take care of it.*

Clarify monitoring: I hope not. To be sure, I'm going to continue to monitor you for the next two months. If there's no further problem, I go away. If the problem continues, you go away. Am I being clear enough?

Re-establish rapport: I'm glad to hear that. As far as any personal problems go, why don't you speak with our personnel manager. There may be something that he can help with or at least recommend some other avenue for assistance.

- **Timing:** After you've observed an abusive pattern—a week, several weeks, a month—move quickly as soon as the behavior occurs again. Publicly ask the employee to come into your office just as he eases back to his work station. You'll have seized control of the dialogue as well as the attention of the other workers who know perfectly well what is going on.
- **Behavior:** Be conspicuous in the work area at a time when the latecomer should be there. As soon as he returns to his desk and sits down, announce you want to meet—right now. Don't wait for a response, just move directly to your office. When he enters, silently gesture him to a seat while you remain engrossed in an open folder of documents clearly visible on your desk. When you're ready to speak, hold the documents up.

ADAPTATIONS

This script can be modified to:
- Deal with the subordinate who wastes time on the job or who is chronically absent, absent on particular days, or late for meetings and deadlines.

KEY POINTS

- When you believe a pattern of behavior is in place, document dates and times.
- Call for your meeting in front of other workers.
- Use physical evidence as a means of reinforcing your position.
- Stay focused on what the behavior has been and its effect on the workplace.
- Do not get side-tracked into debating why the behavior has occurred.
- Be clear about future actions and outcomes.

Correcting Repeated Mistakes by a Subordinate
12.

STRATEGY

Managers are a haberdasher's delight: They have to wear so many hats. Some of these hats are comfortable and complimentary, while others are constraining and tight. Which should you choose to correct a subordinate who makes repeated mistakes? If the worker is new, a comfortable white hat of mentor supporting a fledgling employee is in order. If the subordinate is a veteran, a darker tone might be in order and a headache may loom on the horizon. That's because established workers may see attempts at corrective support as criticism of their performance. The potential for confrontation is ripe. The goal of this script is to help you no matter which hat you choose to wear. The key is your understanding and accepting that your primary role in all interactions with subordinates is supervising successful completion of assigned tasks. That's the head beneath every hat.

TACTICS

- **Attitude:** Your attitude should be confident and authoritative. You are carrying out your role as an effective supervisor. The expertise you share to help solve the problem establishes a position of supportive command.
- **Preparation:** Determine if the mistakes you've observed are random or recurring. Begin to document the mistakes being made. Self–evident mistakes are easy and quick to prove, while less obvious mistakes will take more time and effort to document. Write down the examples that you have seen and keep a record of complaints from others. Review your information to determine the pattern of mistakes. Finally, decide on solutions to correct the problems.
- **Timing:** Convene a meeting as soon as documentation and solutions are established to your satisfaction. However, be aware that a sudden stumble by a veteran employee can be signal of job unhappiness. You need to read this and act quickly.
- **Behavior:** Come out from behind the desk for this meeting and sit with your staff member. That will demonstrate you're interested in helping her solve a problem, not in chastising her for causing one. Clearly present your concerns and documentation and then offer solutions.

47

12. Correcting Repeated Mistakes by a Subordinate

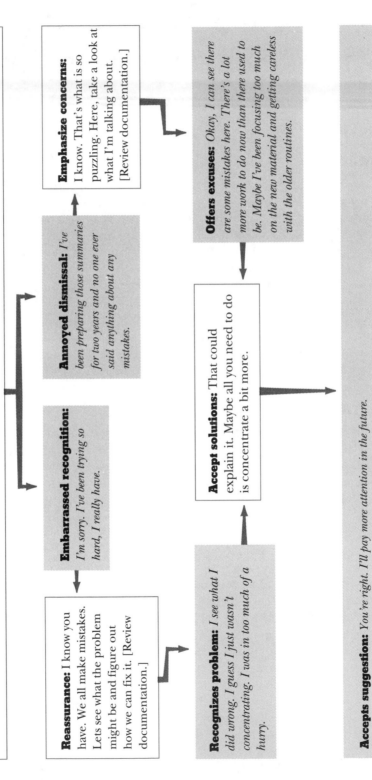

State problem: Pam, the past several weeks there have been similar mistakes in your weekly summaries. Let's take a look at them, see what the problem is, and see how we can fix it.

Embarrassed recognition: *I'm sorry. I've been trying so hard, I really have.*

Annoyed dismissal: *I've been preparing those summaries for two years and no one ever said anything about any mistakes.*

Reassurance: I know you have. We all make mistakes. Lets see what the problem might be and figure out how we can fix it. [Review documentation.]

Emphasize concerns: I know. That's what is so puzzling. Here, take a look at what I'm talking about. [Review documentation.]

Recognizes problem: *I see what I did wrong. I guess I just wasn't concentrating. I was in too much of a hurry.*

Offers excuses: *Okay, I can see there are some mistakes here. There's a lot more work to do now than there used to be. Maybe I've been focusing too much on the new material and getting careless with the older routines.*

Accept solutions: That could explain it. Maybe all you need to do is concentrate a bit more.

Accepts suggestion: *You're right. I'll pay more attention in the future.*

Accepts suggestion: *You're right. I'll pay more attention in the future.*

Establish confidence: I know you can handle the work. Remember, if you have any questions, just ask.

Because the documentation can't lie, expect discomfort and excuses. The intensity of excuse making will be in direct proportion to seniority. A new person will work with you more quickly, but an experienced subordinate will ultimately come around as well.

ADAPTATIONS

This script can be modified to:
- Correct a subordinate who repeatedly ignores required office protocol and procedures.

KEY POINTS

- Approach the problem as a supportive supervisor, not a vindictive snoop.
- Gather documentation that exemplifies the mistakes being made.
- Be ready with solutions to solve the problem, but encourage the employee to come up with her own solution.
- Exhibit confidence in her ability to make corrections.
- Reaffirm your support by offering accessibility to help with future problems.

Putting an End to a Subordinate's Gossiping 13.

STRATEGY

Gossip in the work place is like an open jar of honey: Everyone enjoys a small taste, a big gulp can make you sick, and getting the lid back on is sticky business. Unrelenting, focused attacks on a single worker create fear, resentment, and apprehension in all workers. The gossip monger is rarely called to task by colleagues, protected by the silent shield of everyone's penchant to gossip. The result is the undermining of the equilibrium and effectiveness of the workforce. This script's goal is to put an end to the pronouncements of your office gossip. Your willingness to acknowledge the problem, consider it seriously, and confront the source are the secrets to success.

TACTICS

- **Attitude:** Be firm and confident in your approach. No one will debate that gossip is a good thing. Stress that your intolerance and anger is for the activity, not the person.
- **Preparation:** Try to get actual examples of the gossip's badmouthing. The strength of your documentation will determine if you can, in fact, confront a gossip as the problem or must confront gossip *itself* as the problem. If subordinates come to you to complain, keep notes. Check with other supervisors, too. Your own experiences of negative behavior are a key. Because subordinates may clam up when a supervisor is around, and probably won't snitch on a coworker for an activity they also have engaged in, getting solid documentation may be tough. Still, every work place has a body of common knowledge—everyone just knows—so don't hesitate going with your feelings and instincts.
- **Timing:** As soon as *you* feel satisfied that you've determined who is the primary problem, confront the person. The longer you allow the behavior to continue, the more you send the message that the problem is unimportant. If you delay, you'll have an office gossiping about your lack of concern for an effective, harmonious workplace.
- **Behavior:** Strongly state how professionally destructive and personally repulsive you find the activity. If you have firsthand examples and documentation, confront the person directly and tolerate no excuses. Anger, annoyance at the least, is appropriate. Without documentation, confront the behavior and not the person. Be concerned and solicitous,

13. Putting an End to a Subordinate's Gossiping

Establish control: Peter, we've a serious problem with gossip in the office. It's apparently becoming personal and hurtful.

No evidence: I've gotten reports from a number of people that someone is spreading malicious rumors about the personal life of one of the secretaries. Have you heard anything about this?

Stonewalls: *As you said, gossip isn't anything new or uncommon. But still, I haven't heard about any particularly malicious personal attacks.*

Some evidence: I couldn't help overhearing you holding court by the coffee machine this morning. I know everyone gossips, and I'm not saying you're responsible for the hurtful personal attacks I've learned of, but I wasn't pleased by what I heard earlier.

Denies responsibility: *I'm sorry about that. I didn't mean anything by it. Even though I might have spoke out of turn this morning, I'm not the gossip you're looking for.*

Enlist support: I'm glad to hear that. Because you're very well connected with the rest of the staff, I'd really appreciate your help in solving this problem. Could you spread the word that I'm concerned about this and that I consider personal attacks and gossip to be completely unacceptable? Let everyone know that, whatever the intent, this kind of innuendo is hurtful and unprofessional and will not be tolerated. Can I count on your help in dealing with this situation?

Agrees to help: *Absolutely. I'll spread the word. You can count on me.*

Stress seriousness: Great. Together I hope we can put an end to this problem. Otherwise, I'm going to have to start digging deeper into it and make some serious changes around here. Let me know how it goes.

seeking help from the individual to solve a problem. You'll ultimately win acceptance that the problem is a serious one that can't be tolerated in the workplace. With documentation, you might even get a begrudging acknowledgment of guilt. In either case, be clear what future outcomes will be.

ADAPTATIONS

This script can be modified to:
- Put an end to the antics of the office practical joker and the office know–it–all.

KEY POINTS

- Documentation may not be possible. Move on the problem based on your general knowledge and gut instincts.
- Move quickly as soon as you are aware of it. Do not let it linger.
- Focus on gossip as a harmful and destructive force in the workplace.
- If you've no evidence, ask if the suspect has any and then ask for his help in solving the problem.
- If you've some evidence, reveal it to the suspect and then ask for his help in solving the problem.
- Be clear there will be serious repercussions if the problem doesn't stop.

Reducing the Size
of a Subordinate's Staff

14.

STRATEGY

Downsizing. Streamlining. Doing more with less. Call it what you will, laying off staff is one of the most difficult tasks a manager must perform. Managers often must be the conduit to our subordinates for difficult decisions made by those "upstairs." The goal of this script is to show you how to effectively inform a subordinate she must reduce her staff. The necessity of maintaining the bottom line and the realization that, like it or not, this is one of her responsibilities are the twin pillars that will support your dialogue.

TACTICS

- **Attitude:** You must embody confidence and objectivity. Acknowledge the difficulty of the task at hand, but don't be drawn into dwelling on it. Be businesslike. Focus all efforts on accomplishing a difficult task. Your approach will serve as a model for your subordinate to emulate when she deals with her staff.
- **Preparation:** The most important preparation is making sure all your information is accurate. There can be no question about what must be done, who must do it, when it must be done, and why it must be done. Review the personnel in each of your subordinates' sections because the ultimate recommendation to superiors will be yours. If cuts are being made in specific sections, have the necessary back-up to support their selection.
- **Timing:** Schedule the meeting as soon as possible. Meet first thing in the morning. Establish a "first thing tomorrow" deadline for her recommendation. Tell her you are available throughout the day for clarification and advice. The more rapid her response, the greater time for review and the less time for agonizing and procrastination.
- **Behavior:** Act professional, but recognize the difficulty of the task and be ready to absorb initial objections.

14. Reducing the Size of a Subordinate's Staff

State problem: It's official: We have to downsize our operation. I need a $100,000 salary reduction from your section. Your choices can bring you over that figure, but you can't be under it. I want your recommendations at the start of work tomorrow. Names, salaries, and bulleted reasons for the choice. Prepare this personally and discuss it with no one. Staff reductions are a part of every business. But the more efficiently we do what we have to, the less hurt for everyone.

Seeks alternatives: *That's a lot. Can't we soften that and reduce other places? Supplies? Hardware? Equipment?*

States anxiety: *We're going to lose some good people. This is really going to be tough.*

Questions timeline: *That's really sudden. Can't I have more time to think about this?*

Dispel alternatives: Those were considered. We're near bare bones in some of those areas now. Salaries are our highest expenditure.

Focus on responsibility: I know, but it's part of the job. Make the selections to meet the baseline figure and keep your section functioning effectively.

Justify timeline: The longer we delay, the tougher the job becomes. You know your people. I have confidence that you'll do what is best.

Seeks clarification: *Is my section the only one that's being asked to make these reductions?*

Spread equally: No. I've been given a total figure that I'm spreading equally through the office. Everyone is being hit.

Cuts targeted: Your section is one of two that are being cut. I reviewed the entire department and decided where we could take the hits and still function effectively. I went through the same process I'm asking you to do.

Expresses approval: *That's fair. That will make it a little easier for me to justify.*

Questions decision: *That doesn't seem fair. Why not spread it out over the whole office? That would make it easier on all of us.*

Fairness isn't issue: We have to do what's effective, not fair or easy. I'll be available all day if you need help. Nothing will go upstairs that I haven't reviewed with you and approved.

ADAPTATIONS

This script can be modified to:

- Reduce the size of a subordinate's operating budget or reduce/reorganize job responsibilities.

KEY POINTS

- Be certain facts and figures are accurate and review personnel for each subordinate's section.
- Inform your staff as soon as you know.
- Require rapid turnaround to you. This will limit procrastination and harmful leaks.
- Stress professional responsibilities and job requirements. Don't let personal misgivings interfere with the task.
- Provide support to your staff.
- Be clear that the final recommendations will be yours.

Reducing the Size of a Subordinate's Workspace

15.

STRATEGY

Whether they have one desk among the multitudes, a Dilbert cubicle, or a corner office, individuals take ownership of their workspace. Just look at the photos, pictures, posters, and personal curios that decorate the average workspace. Making a workspace yours creates a sense of comfort. So what to do when workspace must be taken away from a subordinate? Present it as inevitable and not indicative of his perceived value. Expect unhappiness and disappointment. There will probably be some mild resistance and questioning ending in resigned acceptance. If you should face an aggressive and angry response, do not engage in any debate. Restate the facts and offer the chance to go over your head with any concerns.

TACTICS

- **Attitude:** There's no reason to be uncomfortable or to lack confidence. Your conversation will be based on a decision about effective use of space. There will most likely be objective recommendations from experts. Job performance, attitude, or any other individual work traits of the subordinate have nothing to do with the decision. It is, quite literally, a case of "nothing personal." Your manner should mirror this.
- **Preparation:** Keeping your staff informed of your plans is the key. As soon as a decision has been made to add staff, equipment, or machines, let all the affected subordinates know. Emphasize that the changes are improvements that will benefit everyone. Be open about the fact that someone will lose some of his current workspace to make room for this improvement. Assure staff that the physical structure of the workplace will be the basis for determining the area to be modified, nothing else. Tell them when a specific decision has been reached that the subordinate involved will be informed first. Openness builds trust and confidence and underlines that the subordinate losing the space is the object of circumstance, not managerial disapproval.
- **Timing:** As soon as you know, meet with the subordinate. Delaying enables leaks and rumors (which undermine your efforts to be open and fair with all) to start. Remember, everyone is anxious about being the "lucky" choice. Delaying increases the anxiety. Reschedule other business to deal with this.

59

15. Reducing the Size of a Subordinate's Workspace

States action: George, you're going to have to give up part of your office space to make room for the new equipment.

Unhappy acknowledgment: *I knew it. I knew it was going to be me.*

Urges alternative: *Why can't we put the new equipment with our other machines? It would keep it all in one convenient area.*

Emphasizes rationale: Remember, George, it's not you that was selected. It was the area best suited to be modified.

Rebuts alternative: We definitely looked at that. The room is just not there. Our plan gives us the best option to support the effectiveness of the entire staff.

Seeks clarification: *So what exactly does this change mean for me?*

Provide specifics: We're going to move in the wall opposite your door. You'll be giving up about one-third of your space.

Expresses anxiety: *One-third! That seems like an awfully big chunk. It's going to be tight.*

States support: I know. But everything needed to continue as you are will be intact. It will just take some getting used to.

States self-doubt: *It's going to make everything more difficult. I really thought I was doing a good job.*

Reclarifies: Your work is not an issue in any way, George. If someone else was in that office, the same space would be taken. It's the space, not the person in that space.

Accepts situation: *I understand. You have to do what you have to do.*

- **Behavior:** Sit with your subordinate in your office. Removing the official barrier of the desk enhances your image as an understanding supervisor. You sympathize with his unhappiness and understand it, just as you know he understands there is no other choice.

ADAPTATIONS

This script can be modified to:
- Deal with the reassignment of job responsibilities when adding additional staff.

KEY POINTS

- Keep your entire staff well informed every step of the way.
- Be specific about what will happen, why it will happen, and when it will happen.
- Emphasize the change as an improvement for all, acknowledging the hardship for one.
- Affirm that the actions are dictated by architectural necessity and not managerial choice.
- Let the individual affected know as soon as you do. Then let the entire staff know.
- Don't hesitate to encourage a disgruntled subordinate to speak to a superior.

Turning down a Subordinate's Request to Hire His Offspring

16.

STRATEGY

It's difficult to reject a subordinate's family members for employment without the worker taking it personally. To avoid this, you should reinforce her value to the company and make it clear the rejection is clearly a business decision, not a reflection on her. Let her know you share in her disappointment, while at the same time explaining your decision is non-negotiable. Your goal is to help her understand and accept the reasons behind your decision.

TACTICS

- **Attitude:** Be firm, but show understanding and appreciation for an employee who wants to help out her family member.
- **Preparation:** If the employee is asking that you hire a son or daughter for summer work, know what the company's policy and history is on this practice. Also know what your budgetary constraints are. If you're being asked to hire someone full time, know what the applicant's qualifications are, what (if any) positions are open in the company, and what salary range the applicant is looking for.
- **Timing:** Especially in the case of the employee seeking a summer job for a son or daughter, inform her as quickly as possible; they'll need time to look elsewhere. Also, keep in mind that this is a conversation best held at the end of the work day so she can get home and break the news to her child.
- **Behavior:** Show sympathy for what the employee is trying to do; don't sit behind your desk when the two of you talk, nod empathetically when she speaks, and keep eye contact to show your genuine concern. You want her to understand that her request is being rejected, not her.

16. Turning down a Subordinate's Request to Hire His Offspring

Icebreaker: Thanks for coming in, Mary. I received your request that I hire your son, Jack, for the summer. I've met him and I think he's a great kid, but I'm afraid we have no position for him right now.

Veiled suspicion: *Haven't you hired employees' kids in the past? Didn't Bill Wilson's boy work here last summer?*

Plea for sympathy: *But Jack simply has to find a job this summer.*

Personalizes: *Can't you just do this as a favor to me? After all, I've been a faithful employee now for over twenty years.*

Appeals: *I think he'd be terrific out on the loading dock. He'd give you more than your money's worth of work, and you wouldn't even have to pay him benefits.*

Special circumstances: You're absolutely right. You have a very good memory. But Bill's boy was hired only because we received some last-minute orders in April and had both the authority and the money to bring someone on for a few months. That was an extraordinary situation. If that were to arise again, I'd hire your son in a minute. Unfortunately, that's not the case this summer.

No choice: Mary, if your son's work habits are anything like yours, I have no doubt he'd be a tremendous help to us. Unfortunately, I've been given absolutely no money in my budget this year to hire any additional personnel, even on a temporary basis. It's something our company simply can't afford right now.

Anger: *I was counting on you to help us out here. How can you let us down like this?*

Desperation: *Well, I just don't know what we're going to do. We really need to find him a job.*

Support: As I said earlier, Mary, I value you as an employee and I think your son is a fine boy. I've prepared a general letter of reference on his behalf, if you think it would be any help [hand it to her]. I've also checked the want ads in the newspaper. If I were in your position, I think I'd encourage Jack to look at the many seasonal employers in our area—the parks department, golf courses, recreation centers, county pools, that sort of thing. They're always looking for strong, ambitious young men like Jack [stand up].

Absorb anger: I can understand your anger. You assumed I'd be able to give Jack a job and, now that you know I can't, you're worried he's not going to find any summertime work. But maybe I can be of some assistance.

Resigned: *I appreciate the letter, and if you hear of any sort of opening, would you keep Jack in mind?*

Skeptical: *Well, I suppose.*

I'll call: If I hear of an opening he might be suited for, I'll call you immediately. Good luck.

ADAPTATIONS

This script can be modified to:
- Turn down a friend or relative's request to hire her child.
- Turn down an employee's request to circumvent any company procedure.

KEY POINTS

- Be clear at the outset that it is impossible for you to hire the employee's son or daughter, but that it's no reflection on either the child or the employee.
- Reinforce the employee's value to the company.
- Demonstrate your concern by suggesting alternative places of employment.
- Avoid taking responsibility for your employee's anger; make it clear that this is her problem the two of you are addressing, not yours.
- If necessary, stand up to indicate that the meeting is over.
- If the employee is asking you to do a favor by showing her child some form of preferential treatment, make it clear that you simply won't do this, while at the same time reinforcing the employee's value to the company.
- Offer a letter of reference to demonstrate to your employee that you have confidence in her child's abilities.
- Don't make promises you can't keep.

Sending a Voluntary Termination Hint to a Subordinate

17.

STRATEGY

"You can't fire me," legions of sit–com stars have shouted, "I quit!" How often managers wish this cliché could be reality. There are those times when regardless of what efforts everyone has made, an employee just doesn't fit. Attitude, performance, attendance, and all else combine to make it clear that a subordinate just isn't going to make it. The goal of this script is to help you to bring about the voluntary termination of such a subordinate by hinting at its desirability. By presenting evidence of work incompatibility in an understanding, non-threatening manner, soliciting the subordinate's reflection upon that evidence, and indicating the advantages of voluntary termination, hints may become a reality.

TACTICS

- **Attitude:** Expect to feel a bit awkward. As difficult as terminating an employee is, it's still straightforward and businesslike. Hinting to a subordinate that he leave is often uncomfortable because it's so indirect and usually involves a "nice person, poor worker" scenario. Knowing your actions are driven by doing what's best for all should help.
- **Preparation:** Have specific actions and activities that indicate the poor working relationship. Be personally clear on what the advantages of resigning are so you can present them. Finally, carefully prepare and practice the script.
- **Timing:** Meet at least four days before the day you'd actually terminate the subordinate. Schedule the meeting at the end of the work day to allow the employee to think it over overnight and to avoid all-day coworker commiseration that will disrupt the workplace. If your hinting has been successfully "read," or your relationship with the subordinate has allowed you to be direct, meet immediately the next morning to implement the plan.
- **Behavior:** Be controlled and low-key. Because hinting at a course of action is involved, expect questions and confusion, real or feigned, about your position. Even if the message is received, expect being pressed to deliver it more directly. If your rapport with the subordinate allows it, move to being absolutely direct and to the point.

17. Sending a Voluntary Termination Hint to a Subordinate

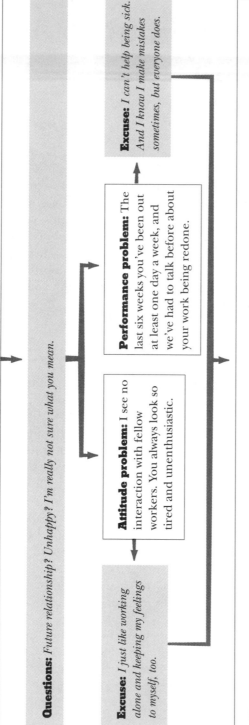

Establish context: Mitch, I'm concerned. You seem very unhappy working here and I worry about your future relationship with the company.

Questions: *Future relationship? Unhappy? I'm really not sure what you mean.*

Attitude problem: I see no interaction with fellow workers. You always look so tired and unenthusiastic.

Excuse: *I just like working alone and keeping my feelings to myself, too.*

Performance problem: The last six weeks you've been out at least one day a week, and we've had to talk before about your work being redone.

Excuse: *I can't help being sick. And I know I make mistakes sometimes, but everyone does.*

Plant seed: Mitch, can you really say you're happy here? Sometimes you look so harried and under pressure.

Explains behavior: *Well, there is pressure; it's work. Sometimes there is just so much to do. It gets to everyone.*

Encourage reflection: Certainly it does. But some handle it better than others. Why continue to be unhappy and under such pressure?

Direct statement: Mitch, the door is closed. This is entirely off the record at this point. But, yes, I'm afraid you are going to be let go. We both know it just isn't working out. Friday is to be your last day. I'd really like to see you resign before then.

Hurt response: *You mean you want me to do the dirty work for you?*

Clarify motives: I want you to get what's best for you in a difficult situation. It looks better to a future employer that you chose to leave, not that you had to be told to leave.

Future concern: *What if I do what you want and a new company checks up on me? What will you tell them?*

Questions directly: *It sounds like you don't want me to work here anymore. Am I going to be fired? Is that it?*

Deflect question: Mitch, at this point I want you to realize you are in control of the situation. You can take actions that are best for you.

Understands situation: *I see what's going on. I'm going to be out, but you would like me to quit so you don't have to fire me.*

Questions motives: *Are you saying you want me to leave? Is that what you want?*

Re-direct challenge: I'm saying people should do what's best for them. They should find a work situation where they feel comfortable and committed.

Set timeline: Think about what we've discussed today and let me know first thing in the morning what you have decided.

Describe support: That you decided to leave on your own also means we can give you a recommendation that could help. You decide how you want this to be done. I'll meet with you first thing in the morning to get your decision.

ADAPTATIONS

This script can be modified to:
- Hint that a subordinate voluntarily relinquish a supervisory role or give up job responsibilities.

KEY POINTS

- Be prepared to give examples of the subordinate's attitude and actions that support your decision.
- Provide enough time before any termination is planned for the subordinate to make a decision.
- Carefully prepare and rehearse what you are going to say.
- Remain low-key but in control and businesslike.
- If the relationship supports it, abandon any hints and be absolutely direct.
- Be clear on your expected timeline for action.

Asking a Subordinate to Improve Her Appearance

18.

STRATEGY

There's no second chance to make a first impression. Even when a business may have a good track record, prospective clients are still greatly influenced by the "what you see is what you get" attitude. A staff that projects a professional appearance can only help build client confidence. A subordinate who doesn't reinforce a "dressed for success" image can only hurt your chances of securing and maintaining clients.

The goal of this script is to help you bring any sartorially challenged members of your staff to the high standard of appearance required as a norm in the world of business. Errant subordinates will try to make this an issue of personal taste because it's really the only argument they can muster. If you're dealing with staff members of the opposite sex, they may even try to lead you into the minefield of gender harassment. That's why you should consider having a fellow supervisor of the same gender as the offender present in your office when you deal with an opposite gender subordinate. This reinforces the professional tone of your position, safeguards potential future misreporting of events or comments, and serves as a role model for proper dress.

Though not absolutely necessary, refer to any print materials distributed previously to employees regarding dress. Don't waiver from your responsibility for maintaining the highest professional standards in the workplace. All possible arguments to justify personal dress shatter against this brick wall position.

TACTICS

- **Attitude:** This problem is visually obvious to any and all, so be confident in confronting it. Given this, project an air of disbelief and disappointment: How could anyone not know how to dress for work! Project this attitude in a clear, matter–of–fact presentation of the problem and the solution. This will underline that your concern is professional, not personal.
- **Preparation:** See if your firm has anything in print regarding appearance: an employee handbook, new employee hand-outs, or recent memos. Check with interviewers to see if they discuss appearance when hiring. Also see if you can get information on how your transgressor dressed for interviews. When you assumed supervisory responsibility of

18. Asking a Subordinate to Improve Her Appearance

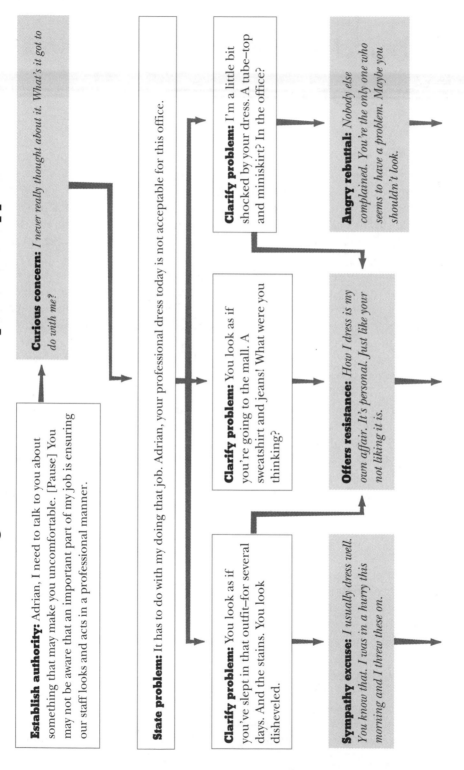

Establish authority: Adrian, I need to talk to you about something that may make you uncomfortable. [Pause] You may not be aware that an important part of my job is ensuring our staff looks and acts in a professional manner.

Curious concern: *I never really thought about it. What's it got to do with me?*

State problem: It has to do with my doing that job. Adrian, your professional dress today is not acceptable for this office.

Clarify problem: I'm a little bit shocked by your dress. A tube-top and miniskirt? In the office?

Angry rebuttal: *Nobody else complained. You're the only one who seems to have a problem. Maybe you shouldn't look.*

Clarify problem: You look as if you're going to the mall. A sweatshirt and jeans! What were you thinking?

Offers resistance: *How I dress is my own affair. It's personal. Just like your not liking it is.*

Clarify problem: You look as if you've slept in that outfit—for several days. And the stains. You look disheveled.

Sympathy excuse: *I usually dress well. You know that. I was in a hurry this morning and I threw these on.*

Offer alternative: I'd rather see you come in a little late with an explanation than look unprofessional.

Refutes argument: No, it's professional. I'd love to dress differently, but I can't anymore than you can. Our jobs demand we look a certain way. Listen, did you dress like this for your interview?

Counter argument: Should I notify our clients and potential clients that they shouldn't look, too? That's absurd.

Embarrassed apology: *I'm really sorry. I understand. I didn't mean any harm.*

Point taken: *Well, uh, no, I didn't.*

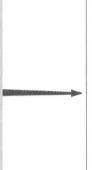

Stubborn deflection: *I don't believe this. I could lose my job because you've got a problem? I have a right to dress any way I want.*

Accepts apology: I'm sure you didn't. That's why I had to talk to you right away. This must not happen again.

Press understanding: Of course you didn't! You wouldn't be here if you did. You dressed to impress us as a professional. I expect that each day.

Assert authority: I'm sure you do. You also have a right to seek work elsewhere if you can't dress as a professional here.

Make outcome clear: If I consider your appearance unacceptable in the future, I'll send you home to change immediately — on your time!

the individual, did you say anything about attire? Make note of all the information concerning the obligation for professional dress in the workplace. This supports your point that appearance is not a matter of any one individual's personal taste but a professional requirement. The proper appearance of fellow workers reinforces this view.

- **Timing:** The instant you see inappropriate dress, move on it. The first time should be the last time. Moving rapidly highlights the importance the problem requires.
- **Behavior:** The moment you observe inappropriate dress, ask to see the individual. Be straightforward in stating the problem. Emphasize that the professional appearance of the staff influences client attitudes and actions. Your concern is, therefore, not a personal one but a professional one that could touch any staff member who does not realize this. You must stick to this and wave your banner throughout: professional not personal!

ADAPTATIONS

This script can be modified to:
- Deal with the subordinate who displays poor hygiene, a subordinate whose work area may be slovenly or inappropriately decorated, or a subordinate whose make-up or jewelry is out of place.

KEY POINTS

- Be familiar with any information given to staff regarding appropriate attire.
- State clearly that the concern involves professional decorum and not personal taste. Maintain this throughout.
- When dealing with a subordinate of the opposite gender, consider having a fellow supervisor of that gender present in your office when you confront the problem.
- Use the individual's interview dress as the key example of what you are after.
- Be specific as to what action you will take if you observe the problem again.

Suggesting a Subordinate Improve His Voice Manners

19

STRATEGY

Every business with a telephone is in telemarketing. Regardless of how technologically advanced the modern office becomes, the telephone remains the instrument for immediate personal contact. No other machine can instantly affect the emotions, attitudes, and perceptions of people. The voices on the company's telephone lines belong to individuals, but what they say speaks for the business. That's why it's important you correct any person whose telephone manners are too informal, too rude, or too vulgar. If you accept it as serious and move rapidly to correct the errant subordinate, the problem can easily be solved.

TACTICS

- **Attitude:** If the staff member is too informal, be businesslike and straightforward but relaxed. Where rudeness or use of inappropriate language is the problem, be annoyed, even angry. They should know better.
- **Preparation:** Have a specific example of the improper behavior. This can be through first-hand experience, or complaints reported to you. You don't need to show the problem is long term and on going. Once is once too often and more than enough reason to move on the situation.
- **Timing:** Meet as soon as you have heard an inappropriate telephone exchange. This emphasizes to all how seriously you regard the behavior. Do the same where a complaint has been made. This is critical when dealing with rudeness or inappropriate language, and desirable in the case of informality. If meeting means cutting into a break or quitting time, so be it. This requires an instant remedy. Summon the person to the meeting over the phone!
- **Behavior:** Be direct and to the point. Where appropriate, convey your annoyance. Stress that rude or vulgar manners are unacceptable in any business. Where informality is the issue, explain why it's a problem, and offer suggestions.

19. Suggesting a Subordinate Improve His Voice Manners

Icebreaker: Kevin, you do a solid job for us. There is, however, a problem I need to discuss with you, one that can be easily fixed. I couldn't help hearing you on the telephone this morning.

Informal: I felt your tone was much too informal.

Rationalizes: *Too informal? I thought that was good. I was trying to make the other person as comfortable as possible.*

Obscene: I heard you using obscene language. You just can't talk on the telephone as if you were in a locker room.

Apologizes: *I really am sorry. I intended no disrespect to anyone. You can be sure this won't happen again.*

Rude: You were being rude and short-tempered, seemingly annoyed. That's as unacceptable on the telephone as it would be face-to-face.

Makes excuse: *I'm sorry. I just lost my temper with some intern who was being a real jerk. Believe me, it's never happened before.*

Strong admonition: You represent this office when you do business with others. Anything less than professional behavior shows disrespect to me, this office, and the person with whom you're talking. The people we work with find great comfort in being treated as professionals. Business calls are just that—business. Understand?

Accepts: *Yes, sir, I do. I'm really sorry. It won't happen again.*

Future outcome: Make sure it doesn't.

ADAPTATIONS

This script can be modified to:

- Suggest improvements to a subordinate's personal interactions or written communications.

KEY POINTS

- Act immediately to confront the problem, especially if rude or inappropriate language is involved.
- Don't be afraid to let your anger show, if necessary.
- Be supportive of a too informal subordinate.
- Accept no excuse for inappropriate behavior or language.
- Emphasize the individual always represents the company.
- Imply future action if the matter isn't resolved.

Handling a
Flirtatious Subordinate

20.

STRATEGY

The overfriendly worker's "hands-on" approach to work coupled with the occasional double-entendre, body brushing, and personal compliments creates one of the most difficult and uncomfortable manager–subordinate problems you'll face. Your success at ending this behavior will depend on your objective, dispassionate approach, citing examples of the behavior. Your focus should be on linking the perceived behavior to the manner in which you and coworkers are adversely affected. Expect responses ranging from anger to embarrassed enlightenment. Don't be surprised at arguments accusing you of sexual harassment and/or male chauvinism. Don't get rattled. Be objective, cite your documentation, and focus on your professional concern for maintaining an effective workplace. Ultimately, it's not important to get agreement: Recognition of your position and the reason for it should be enough to end the problem.

TACTICS

- **Attitude:** You need to be calm and controlled. You're a diplomat who must avoid personal entanglements while dealing with an issue that's clearly personal. Feeling flattered is a natural reaction. But you must maintain the objectivity of a manager who's simply dealing with another workplace problem.
- **Preparation:** Establish that a pattern of behavior is taking place. Keep a record of incidents to confirm not only the problem, but your objective approach to the problem. Include dates to give your notes even more credence. Use fellow managers as sounding boards. If they confirm your observations, so much the better. If they haven't really noticed, ask them to be more aware and give feedback on what they see. Their support is helpful but not absolutely necessary. Your perceptions are enough to initiate action.
- **Timing:** Don't rush into this. The more time you have to document your view, the better. This also gives you a chance to see if the behavior is directed at others as well. Initiate the dialogue at the end of the day, on Friday if possible. This will avoid any co-opting of fellow worker sympathy or anger. It will also offer time for cooling off and reflection.

20. Handling a Flirtatious Subordinate

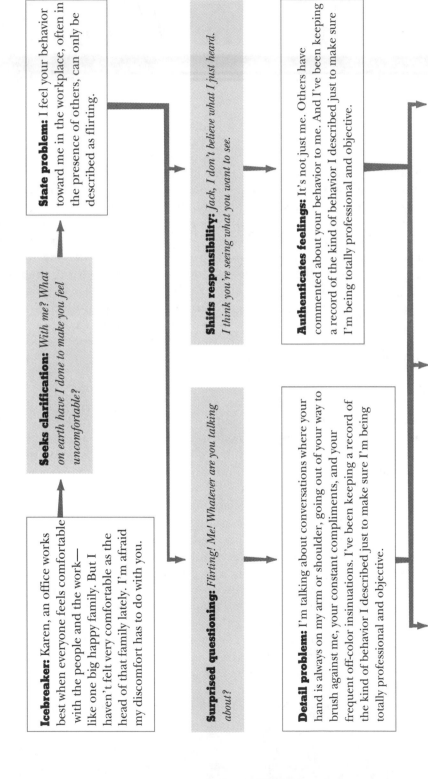

Icebreaker: Karen, an office works best when everyone feels comfortable with the people and the work—like one big happy family. But I haven't felt very comfortable as the head of that family lately. I'm afraid my discomfort has to do with you.

Seeks clarification: *With me? What on earth have I done to make you feel uncomfortable?*

State problem: I feel your behavior toward me in the workplace, often in the presence of others, can only be described as flirting.

Surprised questioning: *Flirting! Me! Whatever are you talking about?*

Shifts responsibility: *Jack, I don't believe what I just heard. I think you're seeing what you want to see.*

Detail problem: I'm talking about conversations where your hand is always on my arm or shoulder, going out of your way to brush against me, your constant compliments, and your frequent off-color insinuations. I've been keeping a record of the kind of behavior I described just to make sure I'm being totally professional and objective.

Authenticates feelings: It's not just me. Others have commented about your behavior to me. And I've been keeping a record of the kind of behavior I described just to make sure I'm being totally professional and objective.

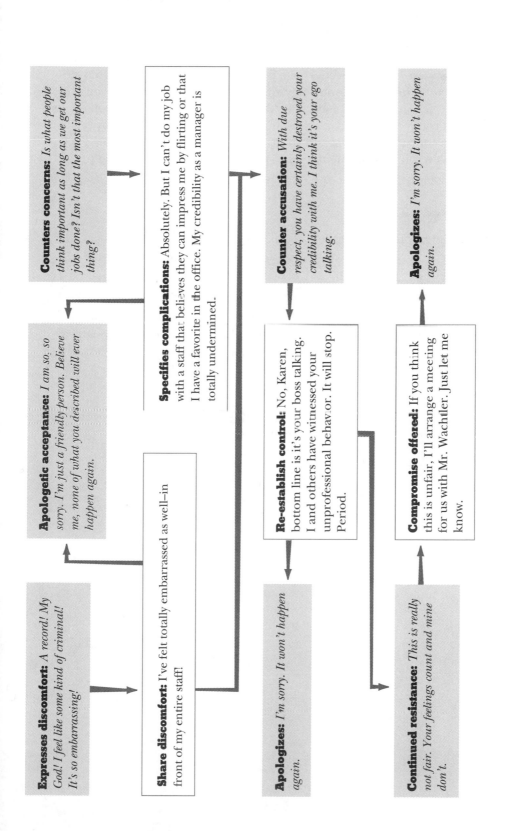

Expresses discomfort: *A record! My God! I feel like some kind of criminal! It's so embarrassing!*

Apologetic acceptance: *I am so, so sorry. I'm just a friendly person. Believe me, none of what you described will ever happen again.*

Counters concerns: *Is what people think important as long as we get our jobs done? Isn't that the most important thing?*

Share discomfort: I've felt totally embarrassed as well–in front of my entire staff!

Specifies complications: Absolutely. But I can't do my job with a staff that believes they can impress me by flirting or that I have a favorite in the office. My credibility as a manager is totally undermined.

Counter accusation: *With due respect, you have certainly destroyed your credibility with me. I think it's your ego talking.*

Apologizes: *I'm sorry. It won't happen again.*

Apologizes: *I'm sorry. It won't happen again.*

Re-establish control: No, Karen, bottom line is it's your boss talking. I and others have witnessed your unprofessional behavior. It will stop. Period.

Continued resistance: *This is really not fair. Your feelings count and mine don't.*

Compromise offered: If you think this is unfair, I'll arrange a meeting for us with Mr. Wachtler. Just let me know.

- **Behavior:** Be the objective manager throughout. Remain at your desk to underline the superior–subordinate relationship. Present your case in a straightforward, matter-of-fact manner. Stay away from comments that could move the conversation onto a personal track. You're dealing with your perceptions, and those perceptions cannot be argued with. You even have documentation of the behavior that shaped the perceptions.

ADAPTATIONS

This script can be modified to:
- Deal with the office flatterer or the favor seeker who provides freebies and all types of small gifts.

KEY POINTS

- Determine that the behavior perceived is part of an on-going pattern.
- Document examples of the behavior to authenticate your perceptions.
- Maintain a tone of professional concern and control at all times.
- Be consciously aware of not responding on a personal level to counter-arguments.
- Meet at the end of the day, on Friday if possible.
- Be clear about what you'll do if the behavior doesn't change.

Suggesting a Subordinate Consider Psychotherapy

21.

STRATEGY

This is an extremely delicate subject to broach because it can generate an enormous amount of defensiveness on the part of your subordinate. In discussing the matter, you need to keep three things in mind: You want to communicate that your primary concern is for the individual's health and happiness, not his productivity; you want to do everything you can to de-stigmatize psychotherapy; and you're not suggesting the employee is "crazy," but overworked, overstressed. That is, he is a perfectly normal person having to cope with extraordinary stresses in his life. The employee's defensiveness will be greatly diminished if he can be made to see the problem as environmental rather than congenital.

TACTICS

- **Attitude:** You want to demonstrate your concern for the employee without seeming alarmist. It's a fine tightrope you have to walk.
- **Preparation:** Know what your company's health plan will cover and know whether the company has an employee assistance program. Be prepared to present options for the employee. Make certain that if your judgment is based on your own observations you have spent sufficient time observing the employee. Have a list of specific behaviors that you've observed.
- **Timing:** This is a conversation best held at the end of the day and the end of the week, so the employee will have the opportunity to digest it and, if necessary, discuss it with family. If possible, you would do well to broach it at a time of the year that isn't particularly busy for your company or the employee. Also, avoid bringing it up any time near the employee's birthday, anniversary, or anniversary with the company.
- **Behavior:** You want to show that your suggestion is meant to be compassionate, not punitive. When the employee comes into your office, welcome him, shut your door, invite him to sit down, and sit across from him in a chair, perhaps with a coffee table separating you. You don't want to be behind your desk (too officious) or right next to him (too threatening).

21. Suggesting a Subordinate Consider Psychotherapy

Icebreaker: Tom, I appreciate your coming in this afternoon. You've always been a conscientious, hard working employee. You do extremely good work. And I believe you care about our company as much as we care about you. Over the past few months, however, I've noticed some distinct changes. Your work isn't as polished, but more important to me, your appearance is often disheveled, you look exhausted, and you're quick to lose your temper. I know this office can be a real pressure cocker, especially for someone as diligent as you. This is why I'd like you to seek an outsider's opinion on what sort of things you can do to manage some of this stress in your life that you're having difficulty handling and I'd like you to see a therapist

Incredulous: *What? I didn't know what you wanted to see me about, but this is the last thing I expected to hear!*

Appeal: *I'll admit I've been a little edgy lately, with the Ackermen account due next week. But as soon as I get that cleared up I promise things will calm down.*

Resignation: *I have been very very tense lately. I didn't know it was so apparent.*

Close the deal: All of us go through high stress times in our lives. In some of those times an outside perspective can really help. I know. I just want you to give it some thought. My door is always open if you'd like to talk.

ADAPTATIONS

This script can be modified to:
- Discuss a worker's possible substance abuse problem.
- Inquire as to whether a worker is having domestic difficulties.

KEY POINTS

- Although you may not be able to order your subordinate to seek counseling, you can apply subtle pressure by letting him know you are concerned with his performance and demeanor.
- You need to walk a fine line. On the one hand, you want him to know you think this is serious. On the other hand, you don't want him to push the panic button. The worker needs to understand that you see him facing a difficult and surmountable problem.
- Understand in your own mind the limits of your own willingness to assist. You may be willing to help the employee find a therapist or even schedule the first appointment. Or, you may feel the need to limit your assistance to this conversation.

Questioning a Subordinate's Expense Report

22.

STRATEGY

When questioning a subordinate's expense report, remember to be calm and collected. The last thing you want is a conversation laced with accusations and denials. If you chastise the employee, nothing productive will arise from the meeting. Your goal is to make the employee aware of a mistake in judgment and be sure it doesn't happen again. Perhaps she took a client out to an expensive dinner or charged the company for an in-room hotel movie. The first example is about judgment and experience. Help the employee recognize the problem and discuss future solutions. In the second example, it's more a question of acceptable behavior. Don't blame her for ordering the movie, just calmly explain it isn't appropriate to charge the company for personal entertainment. If you educate rather than punish, most employees will appreciate your advice and guidance. If the problem persists, you must deal with the employee in a harsher fashion. For a first offense, however, give her the benefit of the doubt and show her how to behave appropriately in the future.

TACTICS

- **Attitude:** Be calm and collected, even friendly. Don't embarrass or accuse the employee. This will only lead to resentment. An upbeat and positive approach will ensure the employee learns from her mistake.
- **Timing:** Have this meeting in private. Never question an employee in front of other workers. Try to schedule the meeting after lunch when the employee will be most relaxed.
- **Preparation:** Anticipate your employee's protests and excuses. Have two copies of the expense report in question. That way you can look over it together.
- **Behavior:** Even if the employee becomes upset at the suggestion of poor judgment or disallowed charges, don't lose your temper. Remind her you're trying to help. Don't threaten her with disciplinary action unless the problem has repeated itself several times.

22. Questioning a Subordinate's Expense Report

Icebreaker: I've been reading over your most recent expense report. There are a couple of items I'd like to discuss with you.

Expensive dinner: I'm glad you took the clients from Acme out to dinner. The bill for dinner, however, was over four hundred dollars. I think that's a little too much for a dinner tab.

In-room movie: I noticed you included the cost of an in-room movie on your expense report. You may not be aware the company does not pay for movies and other entertainment not directly related to work. I'm sure you'll understand if we don't reimburse you.

Blameless: *What was I supposed to do? Ask them to split the check? I had to pay. They're clients, I can't suggest McDonald's for dinner. They wanted an expensive dinner, and I got stuck with the bill. It happens.*

Spin doctor: *We need to keep the client happy. I know the dinner was expensive, but in the long run it's a small price to pay for their business.*

Protests: *C'mon, I'm on a long business trip with nothing to do. I already had a great meeting with Acme, Inc. and I ordered a hotel movie. What's the big deal?*

Apologizes: *I'm sorry. I completely forgot about the movie. I didn't mean to add it to the cost of the room. Sorry about the oversight.*

Explain: Don't get me wrong, I'm glad you took the clients to dinner. Next time, however, be prepared. Do a little research and try to find an affordable restaurant that you can all enjoy. Take control of the situation. That way the client is happy and we don't lose money.

Make your point: Naturally, the client comes first. Next time, however, take the initiative. Suggest an affordable restaurant where the clients will be comfortable. If you take control of the encounter, we can keep the client happy, and save money.

Reason: It's not the cost of the movie that's at issue. It's simply a matter of judgment. Entertainment not pertaining to business shouldn't be charged to the company. I'm sure you understand.

Soothe employee's concern: Don't worry about it. It happens all the time. That's why we have accountants.

Humble: *I understand what you're saying. I'll try to control our future business dinners. I let the situation get out of my control.*

Gives in: *I see your point. I hadn't thought of it that way. It won't happen again.*

Close positively: The only way to learn is from experience.

ADAPTATIONS

The script can be modified to:
- Confront a student about an unintentional cheating incident.
- Coach a worker about appropriate behavior with clients.

KEY POINTS

- Don't lose your temper. It only makes the situation worse.
- Illustrate the error in judgment, thoroughly explain the employee's mistake, and offer possible solutions.
- Remember the goal of the meeting is to educate, not scold. Show your employee the mistake and try to be sure it isn't repeated.
- Don't undermine your employee's confidence. Show you still have faith in her.

Handling a Subordinate's Personal Use of Equipment

23

STRATEGY

Some employees consider office supplies and the machines required for their work as available for their personal use. If paper-clip pilfering adds up, imagine the hidden costs for the worker who thinks "job ownership" means personal use of the firm's copiers, computers, postal machines, telephones, and anything else that plugs into an outlet. When the employee is a highly valued and productive subordinate, some managers look the other way, but this only encourages more of the same. Eventually, personal use of equipment may become so rampant orders will come down from above to crack down hard. That's why it's essential to stop such problems before they attract attention from upstairs.

TACTICS

- **Attitude:** You'll be dealing with behavior you've observed so you can be confident. Be understanding in your approach because the issue is one workers easily rationalize as a job perk, not a problem.
- **Preparation:** The essential element of preparation is validating that abusive behavior is taking place. Your first–hand observations are often enough. But the more effectively you can corroborate those observations with tangible evidence, the more confident you can be of controlling the dialogue and ending the problem.
- **Timing:** Gathering tangible evidence will mean a stronger case, but also more time. When ready, meet at the end of the day. This provides a night of thoughtful reflection and eliminates the potential for day-long gripe sessions with other employees.
- **Behavior:** Project confidence and authority from behind your desk. Have any back-up materials clearly visible and peruse them before speaking. Be authoritative and direct, but not necessarily angry. You don't want to alienate a productive subordinate, but you can't ignore his behavior either.

23. Handling a Subordinate's Personal Use of Equipment

Capture attention: Glen, I'm concerned about a problem I've observed over the last few weeks. You feel perfectly at ease using any of our machines for your own personal needs. [Pointing to papers on desk] If it were just occasional I would say so, but these logs and records show use far beyond what is required for the job. Plus, I've seen it with my own eyes. It's costing us money and must stop.

No big deal: *I make the company a lot of money. I don't think a few copies is a big deal.*

Singled out: *Why are you singling me out? Everyone does this.*

Bottom line counts: You know it's the bottom line that counts. This isn't a charity. Your actions are costing the company money and encouraging others to do the same. Eventually, they'll come to the attention of the people upstairs. This has to stop now.

Own fault: It's the facts that singled you out [hold up papers]. According to these records, you're the biggest offender. I'll speak with others separately, but right now I'm speaking with you. If you don't stop, this behavior will be noticed upstairs. It must stop now.

Acceptance: *Fair enough. I'm sorry. It won't happen again.*

Emphasize confidence: I'm glad to hear that. You're much too savvy a worker to get into more hot water over something like this.

ADAPTATIONS

This script can be modified to:

- Deal with the worker who borrows personal and professional materials from fellow workers.

KEY POINTS

- Be prepared to cite specific incidents based on observation and documentation.
- Do not link the problem to the worker's job performance unless it applies.
- Stay focused on the behavior as a cost factor.
- Be exact in regard to how the problem will be monitored.
- Be clear what the result will be if the problem persists.

Asking if a Subordinate Is a Victim of Domestic Abuse

24

STRATEGY

This is obviously a highly sensitive issue that you must broach with extreme caution, especially if you and the subordinate are of different genders. Be prepared for a tremendous amount of resistance and decide just how far it is useful to push. You may have to settle for half a loaf. Keep in mind that, just by airing the subject, you may be putting the worker on the road to actually addressing it herself later on.

TACTICS

- **Attitude:** You want to show compassion and at the same time maintain a certain distance from the subordinate. Remember that she will be feeling particularly vulnerable and exposed, so it will be up to you to keep some boundaries in place.
- **Preparation:** Read up a little on telltale signs of spousal abuse, such as bruises around the cheeks and eyes, swelling of the lips, and so forth. Also, gather information about local referral services in your community, such as women's shelters, hospitals, police liaisons, clergy, and therapists.
- **Timing:** Schedule a meeting on a Monday, as abuse is often prevalent on weekends. Also, arrange to meet early in the day. If your subordinate agrees to seek help, you want to ensure that there's enough time during that day to get her set up with the proper support system.
- **Behavior:** Meet in your office behind closed doors. Sit at some distance from your subordinate, but not behind a desk. Maintain eye contact, adopt an avuncular demeanor, and display comfort while at the same time pressing the seriousness of the issue.

24. Asking if a Subordinate Is a Victim of Domestic Abuse

Icebreaker: Lois, I appreciate your coming in. Please sit down and make yourself comfortable. [Brief pause] This is extremely difficult for me to ask, but please hear me out. Lois, is there any possibility your husband is physically harming you?

Tears up: [sobs]

Uneasy, slightly indignant: *Why, no. I'm fine at home. Things are just fine.*

Evasive: *Why, uh, no. Well, you know how it is. Jack and I have our disagreements, I suppose, just like any couple. We argue. Sometimes it gets a little heated I guess.*

Angry: *You have no right to ask about my private life!*

Put it in context: I know this is a very private matter. I certainly don't mean to pry and I don't raise this subject lightly. I mention it only because I care about you as a member of this company's family. I've noticed bruises on your face and arms, and you've seemed quiet and withdrawn lately. That's not like the old outgoing Lois, and that's why I'm concerned.

Absorb anger: I understand your feelings, Lois, and I don't bring this up lightly. I only raise it because I care about you, not because I mean to invade your private life. I've noticed your bruises and, frankly, I feel I'd be remiss if I didn't say something.

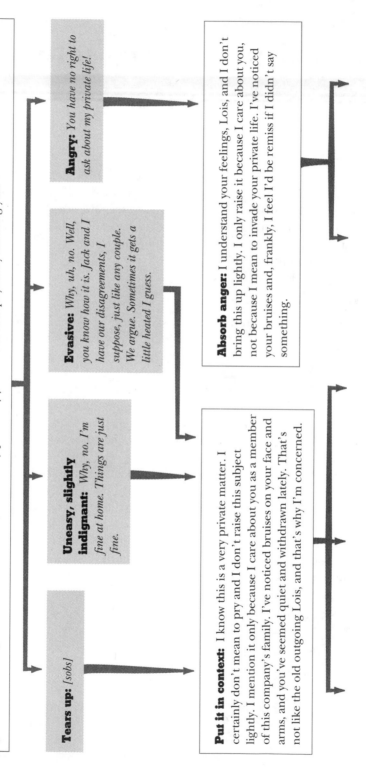

Reluctant: Things have been a little tough lately. Bills have piled up, Jack's dad's been sick, and we've both been really swamped at work. We really do still love each other but, well, it feels like Jack's changed somehow. I don't know; maybe things will get better.

Self-critical: Oh! I was such an idiot for marrying him! My mother was right! I'm so embarrassed. I'm such a jerk.

Self-blame: It's all my fault. I don't get dinner on the table on time. I don't keep the house clean. I know that other wives treat their husbands better, if you know what I mean.

Denial: I don't know what you're getting at. Honestly, I fell down the stairs last week, that's all. [Nervous laughter] I've always been a little clumsy.

Anger: How dare you accuse my husband of beating me! My marriage is just fine, thank you very much! And I'd appreciate it if you'd just mind your own business!

Persuasion and referral: My only concern is your health and well being. I've noticed your bruises and, as I mentioned a moment ago, your mood is very different lately. In the past, the company has referred employees who seemed troubled to a local counselor named Judy Brown. I just want to offer you her card. If you don't need it, who knows, some day maybe you'll know someone who does.

Dismissive: Fine, I'll take her card.

Reluctant: Well, it can't hurt to just talk to her. Okay.

ADAPTATIONS

This script can be modified to:
- Fit the needs of a child who is being abused by a parent (even if the child is an adult).
- Apply to a subordinate who is being psychologically—but not physically—abused by a mate.

KEY POINTS

- You want to make the route from the employee's needs to professional help a path of least resistance, so have resources available and be willing and able to help secure those resources.
- You don't want the employee to come to see you as his or her rescuer; instead, your efforts should be directed toward putting her in touch with professionals.
- Respect the fact that it is often difficult for abuse victims to admit even to themselves that abuse is occurring. Their resistance to admitting it to someone outside their own immediate circle of friends and family will only be stiffer. Your goal should be to at least send the employee out of your office with the business card of a resource person. The employee may indeed want to take steps to resolve the problem, but not in front of you.

Dealing with a Brownnosing Subordinate

25

STRATEGY

If the faint praise of a subordinate makes you uneasy, then intense praise will make you sick. The workplace brownnose who trumpets your praises no matter what you do is actually undermining your credibility and authority. The public nature of extravagant flattery, often in your presence, adds embarrassment to the mix. The longer the praise goes on, the more you risk having other subordinates believe this is how to impress you and is what you value in the workplace. Expect an initial response of shock and surprise to your efforts. Next will be pleas of innocence, not for his actions, but for his intent. He may even try to brownnose you in this meeting! That's why you must be unrelenting in emphasizing that it is the perception of his actions and comments that is destructive, regardless of his intent.

TACTICS

- **Attitude:** You should be offended and annoyed by brownnosing behavior. Such a subordinate is calculating and shallow and implies to others by his actions that you may be the same. A subordinate who thinks you'll be impressed by transparent praise and unsought personal attention is insulting your integrity and should make you angry.
- **Preparation:** Be ready to refer to the instances the subordinate's behavior made you feel uncomfortable, why you felt uncomfortable, and the affect on others. Don't worry about exact times and dates, just make a list from your own memory. Highlight any daily or weekly pattern of brownnosing rituals. If other managers have commented to you about your unwanted office buddy, include their observations and comments.
- **Timing:** When your gut tells you you're a target, act. An ideal time to do so is immediately following a public display by the "suck up."
- **Behavior:** Turnabout is fair play in the embarrassment department. By initiating your dialogue publicly, you'll also demonstrate your annoyance to other subordinates.

25. Dealing with a Brownnosing Subordinate

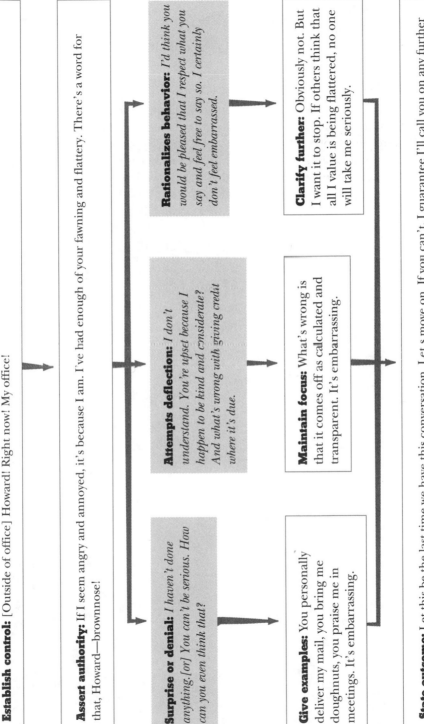

Establish control: [Outside of office] Howard! Right now! My office!

Assert authority: If I seem angry and annoyed, it's because I am. I've had enough of your fawning and flattery. There's a word for that, Howard—brownnose!

Surprise or denial: *I haven't done anything. [or] You can't be serious. How can you even think that?*

Give examples: You personally deliver my mail, you bring me doughnuts, you praise me in meetings. It's embarrassing.

Attempts deflection: *I don't understand. You're upset because I happen to be kind and considerate? And what's wrong with giving credit where it's due.*

Maintain focus: What's wrong is that it comes off as calculated and transparent. It's embarrassing.

Rationalizes behavior: *I'd think you would be pleased that I respect what you say and feel free to say so. I certainly don't feel embarrassed.*

Clarify further: Obviously not. But I want it to stop. If others think that all I value is being flattered, no one will take me seriously.

State outcome: Let this be the last time we have this conversation. Let's move on. If you can't, I guarantee I'll call you on any further brownnosing on the spot. I won't care who's present. Now show me by your actions that neither of us needs to be made uncomfortable again. That's all.

ADAPTATIONS

This script can be modified to:

- Deal with the giver of unsolicited gifts and office freebies.

KEY POINTS

- Initiate dialogue immediately after an incident takes place.
- Make a list of examples of incidents from memory, highlighting patterns.
- Be direct and forceful.
- Stress the debilitating effect such behavior has on others.
- Focus on job performance as the way in which a subordinate can impress you and gain respect.

Apologizing to a Subordinate for Your Own Behavior

26.

STRATEGY

In apologizing to a subordinate, you are in essence turning the tables on the power dynamic that exists between the two of you. A dicey proposition, you can use it to your advantage by demonstrating that you're not too big to admit when you've made a mistake. You also want to be clear about what you're apologizing for. For instance, you may have had every right to be angry with a subordinate for something she did or failed to do, but now regret the severity of your tirade.

TACTICS

- **Attitude:** Show honest contrition and a willingness to admit your mistake. But don't blur the distinction between boss and subordinate. Don't grovel.
- **Preparation:** Before meeting with the worker, make sure you've calmed down sufficiently and composed yourself adequately. Go over this script in your head; know what you want to say. Go to her office and tell her you want a moment of her time.
- **Timing:** Ideally, you want to have this conversation on the same day the behavior occurred. You also want enough time to elapse so that you've had opportunity to cool down and the subordinate has recovered from the blow. But you don't want to wait too long; feelings will just fester. Getting on top of this quickly will be appreciated by the aggrieved.
- **Behavior:** Be firm, confident, and relaxed. Be prepared for some anger and resistance and don't surrender to any desire you might have to react impulsively. More important than making sure your apology is accepted, you want to make sure it's heard. Also, if necessary, at the end of the dialogue, reassert your status as this person's superior, perhaps by requesting some work from her.

26. Apologizing to a Subordinate for Your Own Behavior

Icebreaker: Hi, Michelle. I just need a minute of your time. I want to apologize for blowing up at you the way I did this morning. I'm terribly sorry.

Gracious: *Well, I appreciate that. Apology accepted.*

Angry: *You should apologize to me! I didn't deserve to be spoken to that way and I didn't appreciate it!*

Retaliatory: *Actually, I've asked for an appointment with Mr. Quimby [your supervisor]. I think he should know how you treated me.*

Icy: *I'd rather not discuss it right now. I have a lot of work to do.*

Appreciation: I appreciate your accepting my apology. It wasn't at all like me to explode the way I did, and if you don't mind, I'd like to explain why it happened.

Absorb anger: You have every right to be angry. My explosion was out of proportion. I was unhappy with the way you handled the McKenna account and I overreacted.

Persist: I certainly understand how you feel right now, but I need to take a minute to explain myself and I think you need to hear me out. You and I have enjoyed a very healthy relationship and it's important that we air this out.

Amenable: *Well, okay, but there's really nothing you need to say.*

Icy: *All right.*

Reluctant: *Okay, but don't think this is going to change my mind.*

Resistant: *I said, I don't want to discuss it*

Patient: That's fine. But if nothing else, then, I want you to please listen to what I have to say.

Explanation: I think you know that our department has been under enormous pressure lately. I've been quick tempered with a few people today and, when I discovered you'd lost McKenna, I just blew. I got angrier than I should have, I'm sorry, and I can assure you it won't happen again.

Still angry: *Look, you still shouldn't fly off at me like that!*

Stonewalling: *Yeah, you certainly did blow up.*

Going upstairs: *Well, I may need to talk with Mr. Quimby.* [your superior]

Agreeable, understanding: *I understand. And I'm sorry about McKenna.*

Supportive: I understand. In fact, I went to see him myself this morning. I had to tell him about McKenna and I also wanted him to know how I overreacted. He supported my suggestion that I come talk with you about what happened.

Absorb anger, bring closure: I think we're in agreement on that. I thought it would be helpful for both of us if you had my explanation [stand to leave]. Now I think it's time we both get back on the ball and see if there's any chance we can get McKenna back in the fold [smile, offer a handshake]. I'd appreciate getting your thoughts on that tomorrow.

Closure: I'm glad you understand. This has been helpful.

ADAPTATIONS

This script can be modified to:

- Apologize for wrongly accusing a subordinate of some form of malfea-sance.
- Apologize for chastising an employee in front of her colleagues.

KEY POINTS

- Be very clear about what you're apologizing for. You didn't harass your subordinate. You didn't unfairly single her out. You overreacted.
- Don't be hesitant about gently reminding the subordinate that she was being reprimanded for a mistake she made.
- Behave like an employer even when you're apologizing. Keep control over the discussion by making sure your subordinate listens to what you have to say.
- Make certain you have the last word.

Turning down a Subordinate's Request for Time Off

27

STRATEGY

As a manager, you're no doubt aware the easiest way to earn a reputation as a bad guy is to say "no" to a subordinate without being able to give him a good, solid reason for your refusal. However, if you can legitimately back up your rejection, you've a chance of coming across as a human being while still maintaining managerial control of the office. When a valued, hard-working employee has already used up all his sick/personal time, you must be clear in your own mind as to what you and the company consider legitimate reasons for additional time off. For example, time off for a doctor's appointment or having to close on a home purchase might be acceptable: Both events must be scheduled during business hours and are important. On the other hand, time off for sports events or taking a son to look at a college shouldn't be acceptable because these are activities that easily can be taken care of on the weekend and aren't essential. If your subordinate's request is legitimate, the only reason you can give for turning him down is that his timing is bad: Things are simply too busy at work for you to let him have that day off . . . at least not without compensation time. If you feel his request is unacceptable, your tack will be to invoke precedent, as in, "If I let you have the day off to go to the Monster Truck Rally, before you know it I'll have everyone coming in here asking for days off." Just remember: Whatever your personal feelings about the employee and his request, the language of your refusal must pertain to business, period.

TACTICS

- **Attitude:** While your first instinct might be annoyance, try to keep an open mind and be fair. Let him state his case and then decide accordingly.
- **Preparation:** Although each request for time off must be handled individually, you can expedite the process greatly by knowing what you and the company consider valid reasons for time off and reasons that are beyond the pale.
- **Timing:** Unfortunately, this is one request you're likely to be blind-sided by: One minute you're sitting in your office working, the next you've got a subordinate poking his head around the door asking if he can have a word with you. If you can handle it there and then, great. However, if

27. Turning down a Subordinate's Request for Time Off

His opener: *Mr. Burns, may I speak with you a minute?*

Polite response: Sure, Steve. What's up?

Legit reason for time off: *I need to know if I can have Friday off to go to the doctor. I know I've used up my sick and personal days, but Friday is the only day I could get an appointment to see her and I'm having some tests done that require me to fast for 24 hours beforehand.*

Bogus reason for time off: *It's my kid. He wants to go to Springfield U next year, and I thought maybe I could take Friday off, beat the traffic, and take him up there to have a look around.*

Thumbs up: We're not under any time pressures right now so . . . sure, no problem. Make sure you let me know how everything turns out, okay?

Time pressure: Normally, it wouldn't be a problem. But as you know, that report absolutely has to be on Jenkins' desk on Monday, and I need you to be here. Would it be possible for you to try to reschedule?

Thumbs down: Springfield U is a great school, but unfortunately, company policy doesn't allow time off for parents who want to take their children to look at colleges. If I let you do it, everyone will want to do it. I'd suggest you just leave after work on Friday or early Saturday morning.

Can't reschedule: *The problem is, I really had jump through hoops to get this appointment and, even then, I'm lucky they're squeezing me in. I know the timing is bad, but I really need to see the doctor.*

Our secret: *No one else but you has to know why I'm not here on Friday.*

Being unfair: *You gave Jackson a day off to take his mother to look at nursing homes.*

Suggest comp time: If you can't reschedule, you could stay late on Thursday and come in on Saturday morning. I'd have no problem with you taking Friday off if you guarantee that report will be on Jenkins' desk first thing Monday morning.

Stick to your guns: I'll know why you're not here, and it's not my policy to lie for employees. How about this? If you can get your work done on time, you can leave an hour early. But there is no way I can give you the entire day or even half the day. There's simply too much to do.

Not comparable: I gave Jackson the day off because that was an emergency situation that could not be rescheduled. You may not have known this, but Jackson stayed late three nights in a row to be able to take that day off.

Will try to reschedule: *I'll see what the doctor's office says about rescheduling and get back to you.*

Should have lied: *Are you saying I should have lied to you, maybe told you I had to go to the doctor?*

Honesty is the rule: No, I'm saying there are valid reasons for taking time off and there are invalid reasons for taking time off, especially when you've run out of sick days and personal days. If you actually had a doctor's appointment, I've no doubt we could work something out. However, lying isn't the way to behave in the workplace.

Agrees: *I'll be here Thursday night and Saturday morning and the report will be on Jenkins' desk Monday morning. I promise. Thank you.*

you can't, ask him to stop by after work or set up an appointment for the following day when he might speak to you in your office. If he corners you in the hallway, do the same.

* **Behavior:** Be polite, attentive, and sympathetic. Stop what you're doing when he makes his case and maintain eye contact. Don't interrupt. You're his boss, not the Grand Inquisitor, so avoid playing 20 questions. Whatever your personal feelings about the request, don't roll your eyes, sigh heavily, or chuckle. No one likes to be belittled.

ADAPTATIONS

This script can be modified to:

* Deal with a spouse or child seeking release from an obligation.

KEY POINTS

* Before a conversation even takes place, have a clear sense of what you and the company consider legitimate as well as unacceptable reasons for time off.
* If the request is legitimate, but the timing is poor, simply tell him he can't have the time because he's needed at work.
* If the request is unacceptable, tell him you can't give him the time for that kind of reason and say it would set an unwanted company precedent.
* Be fair and open–minded about suggestions for compensation time.

II

Lifescripts

...for Superiors

Asking Your Superior 28. for More Staff

STRATEGY

If you're in charge of a department that needs more staff yet you know your company either cannot or will not hire more people, you'll need to convince your superiors to let you poach staff from other departments. Not only do you need to make a strong argument for why you can't get by with the staff you have, but you also have to justify how the department you're poaching from can get by without them. Make your reasons and rationales as factual as possible and as closely tied to the specific individuals involved as possible. Emphasize the benefits to the company as a whole. Realize this could be perceived as a power play by your boss and will be resented by the manager of the department from which you're poaching. That's why your reasons for the shifts must be beyond reproach.

TACTICS

- **Attitude:** Your department is doing well, but could be doing even better. What you are proposing will boost profits, not only for your department, but for the whole company. It's an idea that makes the most sense under the current staff restrictions.
- **Preparation:** Figure out who you can poach and from where. Develop a rationale for the shift. Decide whether you want this to be temporary or permanent, realizing that temporary shifts will be much easier to achieve.
- **Timing:** This is a tough call. The need for the added bodies must be near enough to be apparent, but the more time you allow for the shift, the more apt you are to get it. You'll need to use your judgment.
- **Behavior:** Be upbeat and positive. You've come up with a proposal that makes more money for the company and that benefits everyone. Don't be defensive—this isn't a power play. Be flexible and open to suggestions: Your goal is to improve your department's efficiency so any steps made in that direction are positive.

2.1. Asking Your Superior for More Staff

Icebreaker: I've been trying to figure out how to increase my department's and the company's bottom line and I've come up with a solution that won't cost the company anything.

Bites: *I'm all ears.*

Pitch: I'd like you to shift Jones and Rodriguez from the Midwest department to my department.

What about other departments?: *Everyone is understaffed right now, including the Midwest. If I let you poach people, I'll just be robbing Peter to pay Paul.*

Other department justification: The Midwest is down 25 percent this year; I'm up 25 percent. They don't have enough work for all their salespeople; I've got more than my staff can handle.

Why do you need them?: *I don't see how two more staffers will help your department. You've got enough staff right now.*

Justify own need: Our business is up more than 25 percent this year, and we were understaffed before the increase. I can't keep up the level of customer service that's led to this increase without more sales people.

Sets bad precedent: *If I let you get away with that, everyone will be poaching from everyone else—it will be open season to steal from other departments.*

Not bad precedent: Not necessarily. If the reason for the shift were made clear, it would just demonstrate that the company is flexible enough to allocate its resources wherever they're needed.

Questions individual choices: *Do Jones and Rodriguez know enough about Eastern accounts to make a difference?*

Individuals' qualifications: Jones spent two years as a sale assistant in the Eastern department, and Rodriguez handled the Eastern region for Acme before he came here to work for us.

Questions individuals' morale: *Are you sure Jones and Rodriguez are going to be happy moving from Cincinnati to Boston?*

Individuals' motivation: After they see the opportunity to make more money out here in the East, I'm sure they'll have their bags packed.

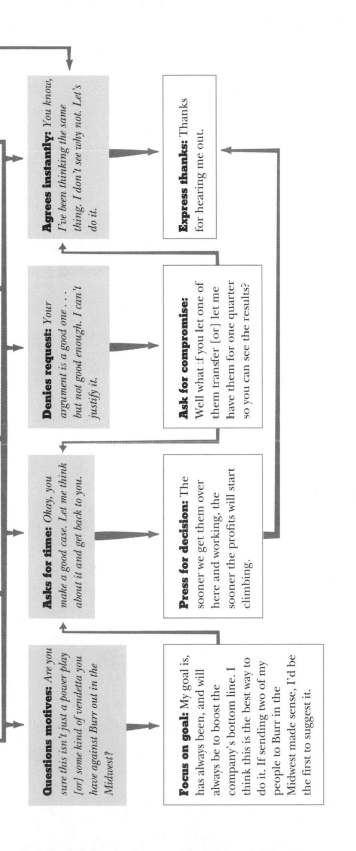

Questions motives: *Are you sure this isn't just a power play [or] some kind of vendetta you have against Burr out in the Midwest?*

Asks for time: *Okay, you make a good case. Let me think about it and get back to you.*

Denies request: *Your argument is a good one . . . but not good enough. I can't justify it.*

Agrees instantly: *You know, I've been thinking the same thing. I don't see why not. Let's do it.*

Focus on goal: My goal is, has always been, and will always be to boost the company's bottom line. I think this is the best way to do it. If sending two of my people to Burr in the Midwest made sense, I'd be the first to suggest it.

Press for decision: The sooner we get them over here and working, the sooner the profits will start climbing.

Ask for compromise: Well what if you let one of them transfer [or] let me have them for one quarter so you can see the results?

Express thanks: Thanks for hearing me out.

ADAPTATIONS

This script can be modified to:

- Respond to a superior's request to improve your department's productivity.
- Request a greater share of supplies or resources for your department.

KEY POINTS

- Be prepared to justify your request as far as your department, the other department, the company, and the individuals are concerned.
- Be prepared to negotiate for a partial shift.
- Emphasize the positive impact on the company, not your department.
- Prepare to defuse any charges of power grabbing.

Asking Your Superior for a Budget Increase

29

STRATEGY

Asking for an increased budget is the ultimate uphill battle in today's lean business environment. Still, it can be done . . . as long as you frame it properly. The secret is to present the budget increase as a proactive effort to take advantage of an already existing opportunity, resulting in an improvement to the company's bottom line. That means it will boost revenues more than it will increase costs. It cannot be seen as a reaction to prior cuts, an attempt for more personal power, a totally new concept, an effort to save time, or as a drain on the company's coffers. Be aware that asking for an increased budget carries risks whether you get it or not. If you achieve your goal, you'll be under increased scrutiny. If you don't achieve it, you may be marked as being out of step.

TACTICS

- **Attitude:** Whatever the real circumstances underlying your request, the attitude you bring to the meeting must be one of excitement and hope, rather than despair and exasperation.
- **Preparation:** Develop an ironclad business plan that documents how your proposed change will have a positive impact on the bottom line. Make sure there are no loopholes or question marks. In addition, have a host of fallback positions ready in case you're unable to overcome your superior's objections
- **Timing:** Don't wait for budget time to present your plan. If you do, it will simply be seen as an effort to grab a bigger piece of the pie or to maintain what you've already got. Instead, present your plan as soon as you've got all your documentation ready.
- **Behavior:** Act the same as in every other planning meeting you have with your supervisor. Remember: You're not asking for more money, you're demonstrating there's an opportunity to make more money, and you're urging the company to take advantage of it. Refrain from suggesting cuts elsewhere, even if you're pushed. That will color your proposal as political.

2.2. Asking Your Superior for a Budget Increase

Icebreaker: Thanks for seeing me. I think I've figured out a way for us to dramatically increase the net revenue generated by my department.

Pitch: By adding a sales position dedicated to classified sales, my figures show we can increase gross revenue by more than 40 percent with only a 10 percent increase in overhead. That translates into a substantial boost in our profitability. Take a look at this.

Attacks you: *Aren't you talking about something you should have done yourself? [or] Aren't you just trying to add to your power base?*

Too long term: *Maybe you're right. But it looks like it could take a couple of years for it to pay off. We're not in the position to make any long-term investments now.*

Don't have money: *You might be right. However, we just don't have the money to gamble on something like this right now.*

Against grain: *Haven't you been reading the papers? The last thing anyone is doing these days is adding staff [or] increasing budgets. It's out of the question.*

Company's first: I'm surprised. The company has always been what's most important to me. I thought you wanted suggestions. If you think I'm doing this for myself, you're mistaken.

Do it half way: I've thought of that. There are a couple of ways we could get instant results. We could hire a part-timer or we could start off with a temp.

Cut to add: I think we can eliminate the risk by temporarily cutting back 10 percent on our T&E budget. That way the new move will pay off from day one.

An opportunity: I'm aware this is against the grain, but everyone's also saying take advantage of openings. I don't think we want to spite ourselves just because of a trend.

Outline plan: I've prepared this memo. In it I've got a two–year, monthly profit and loss for the change I'm suggesting. I've validated all the assumptions. I'd like you to look at it. Of course, I'm willing to make any modifications you'd suggest before kicking it upstairs.

Open to idea: *All right, let's go over what you have in mind.*

Still against idea: *I'm sorry. I just can't bring that kind of suggestion upstairs.*

Ask for reconsideration: Let me leave this memo with you. In it I've got a two-year, monthly profit and loss for the change I'm suggesting. I've validated all the assumptions. Just take a look at it. I think you'll reconsider when you see the numbers. I'll get back to you tomorrow.

ADAPTATIONS

This script can be modified to:
- Ask for an assistant.
- Ask for a new piece of equipment.

KEY POINTS

- Frame your proposal as "an opportunity," explain that you've just "uncovered" it, and stress, as early in the conversation as possible, that it will boost net revenues.
- If your supervisor attacks you and suggests the proposal is self serving, act surprised and hurt, but not angry, and stress you've always put the company first.
- If your supervisor objects to even a short–term negative impact on the bottom line, provide temporary options that will offer instant positive results.
- If your supervisor objects to any additional outlay, suggest temporary shifts in your own operations to compensate.
- If your supervisor says your idea is counter to current trends, show how it's really in line with today's business philosophy.
- If your supervisor remains hesitant, ask him to think about it and reconsider. Meanwhile, consider going over his head.

Warning Your Superior of Potential Client Problems

30

STRATEGY

Be cautious when delivering the news of a potential client problem. You need to tell your superiors you have a feeling, call it intuition, that Acme, Inc. may be preparing to pull its business. The fear is your superiors will react poorly and blame the messenger. Deliver the news and assume control of the meeting right away. If your superiors have a chance to vent anger, lay blame, or panic, the possibility of accomplishing something productive will be lost. Concentrate on moving the conversation forward and searching for a solution to the client problems. If you can demonstrate calm under fire, your superiors will think of you as a valuable employee. This is your chance to help the company avoid losing a client and make an effective impression. Devise a plan of action to share with your superiors during this potential crisis. Before they have time to point fingers, you can steer them toward a discussion about how to deal with the problem. Get them involved in the discussion, seek their opinions, and force them to comment on your thoughts and ideas for handling the client. Don't discuss who's at fault, but subtly prove you're not to blame for this situation. You're trying to help the company avoid a problem, not throwing yourself at the mercy of your superiors. By meeting with your superiors, you're taking a proactive stance and thus protecting yourself from future recrimination. If Acme pulls their business without any warning, you will be held accountable. If you warn your superiors of the potentially volatile situation, you will be recognized as a team player who is watching out for the well-being of the company.

TACTICS

- **Attitude:** Be quick and decisive. Seize control of the dialogue and make the group search for a solution. Force a discussion of potential defenses and counter maneuvers to the client problem.
- **Timing:** Meet with your superiors soon after you sense there's a problem. Don't race into a meeting half cocked. Meet with them as soon as you have control of your emotions and feel able to explain the situation in a clear and coherent fashion.
- **Preparation:** Organize your thoughts and prepare notes about the problem. Try to rehearse a quick and effective speech to begin the meeting. Formulate ideas for dealing with the situation and be ready to share your thoughts during the meeting.

2.3. Warning Your Superior of Potential Client Problems

Icebreaker: Thanks for meeting with me on short notice. I have a feeling that Acme may be preparing to pull their business. They haven't said anything directly, but I have a strong sense that something is wrong. Just to be on the safe side, I think we should discuss possible plans of action.

Gets angry: *How the heck did this happen? What did your team do? Acme is an important client, and we can't afford to lose them. If we do, heads are going to roll.*

Panics: *If we lose Acme, we're in a heap of trouble. We need their business. What are we going to do about this? What did they tell you? What did they say?*

You're paranoid: *I think you may be overreacting. You say you only have a sense. If they haven't said anything to indicate they're unhappy, then I don't think we should lose sleep over this.*

Remains calm: *Can you tell me why you have this feeling? If we can identify the problem, we'll have a better chance of rectifying the situation.*

Redirect anger: I believe something is wrong at Acme. We need to find out what the problem is and address it head on. I propose we arrange a meeting with the partners of Acme to address any issues.

Soothe panic: If we react swiftly, we may not lose their business. We need to reevaluate our working relationship and address any problems. If we arrange a meeting with the partners at Acme, I think we can clear the air and get to the bottom of this.

Cautious, not paranoid: I think it would be a big mistake to ignore this problem. It can't hurt to meet with the partners at Acme. At the very least, they will appreciate our personal attention and it will solidify our working relationship.

Explain: As I said, it's nothing concrete, just a feeling. Still, I think we should prepare ourselves. I propose we meet with the partners of Acme. We can tell them we just want to review our working relationship.

Still angry: *Maybe if we knew who the heck screwed up or at least what's wrong we could fix the problem. What are we supposed to do? Sit down with the people from Acme and say we have a feeling something is wrong?*

Wants elaboration: *What would the meeting you propose accomplish? We can't exactly sit down and ask what's wrong. We could end up looking foolish.*

Not convinced: *I still don't see a problem. Let's wait a couple of weeks and see what happens. If you get any concrete evidence that Acme is going to pull their business, we can talk again. Until then, let's stick to business as usual.*

Solve the problem: We can tell them the meeting is about reviewing our working relationship. If they feel something is wrong, they're more likely to air their concerns in this forum. We'll be demonstrating our dedication to their business and seeking the solution to their problem.

Disagrees: *I don't think a meeting is necessary. We may give them a sense of power in our relationship. We don't want to show too much of our hand. Let's just play along for a while and see what happens. If you hear anything, let me know.*

Protect yourself: I understand your position. Just as a precaution, I'm going to prepare a brief memo outlining the possible reactions to an Acme pull out. I'll write the memo in my free time. Thanks for taking the time to meet with me.

Agrees: *All right, I guess I can't see a down side. You'll coordinate with our group and theirs. Find a good time for a brief meeting. I want you to personally arrange everything.*

Express thanks: I'll handle all the arrangements. I'm sure this meeting will heal any wounds with Acme. Thanks for hearing me out and addressing this situation.

- **Behavior:** Be confidant. You are racing to the rescue of the company. Move the conversation swiftly and remind your superiors the most important thing to do is address the situation.

ADAPTATIONS

This script can be modified to:
- Protect yourself from a destructive peer.

KEY POINTS

- Guide the conversation toward a solution. Don't let it degenerate into a finger–pointing melee.
- Don't accept blame for the situation. You have a feeling, but it's not your fault.
- Suggest meeting with the client and trying to get them to air any grievances. Even if they don't have a problem, the meeting will be a boost to your working relationship.
- If your superiors don't heed your warning, offer to prepare a memo outlining possible reactions to a client pullout. This will further protect you from recriminations.

Warning Your Superior of Potential Vendor Problems

31

STRATEGY

If you learn a vendor your company relies on may be about to run into trouble either with their own operation or in servicing your company, you need to alert your superiors. However, you'll first need to take certain things into consideration. What's the likelihood that vendor service will be interrupted and how long will it be for that to happen? What are the alternative sources for the goods or services, and what are their relative strengths and weaknesses? Does the problem have to do with the workings of your own company or its relationship with the vendor? The reason for all this preliminary thought is that you want to provide some advice on a potential course of action. However, remember that the problems you foresee may not arise. If your company goes through a costly or time–consuming shift that wasn't necessary, you'll be blamed—just as if you hadn't noticed the problem at all.

TACTICS

- **Attitude:** You've noticed something that may be harmful, but because you've noticed it early, the company has the opportunity to proceed with caution. That means not rushing to judgment or taking action, although the more people you make aware of the problem the better.
- **Preparation:** Thoroughly analyze the problem and the potential solutions, coming up with a list of alternative responses, both now and in the future. Choose one response because you may be asked for a specific recommendation.
- **Timing:** Time may not be of the essence, but the longer you delay the less of an advantage your foresight will seem. Present the problem as soon as you've gathered all your facts and have formulated your own opinions. Don't schedule an emergency meeting or interrupt regular business—just ask for the next available time slot.
- **Behavior:** While this isn't good news, the fact that you saw the potential for it happening before it did gives your company a competitive advantage. Don't gloat, but don't shy away from credit. Try to walk the middle ground between alternatives unless the evidence clearly points to one solution or unless you're forced to choose.

2.4. Warning Your Superior of Potential Vendor Problems

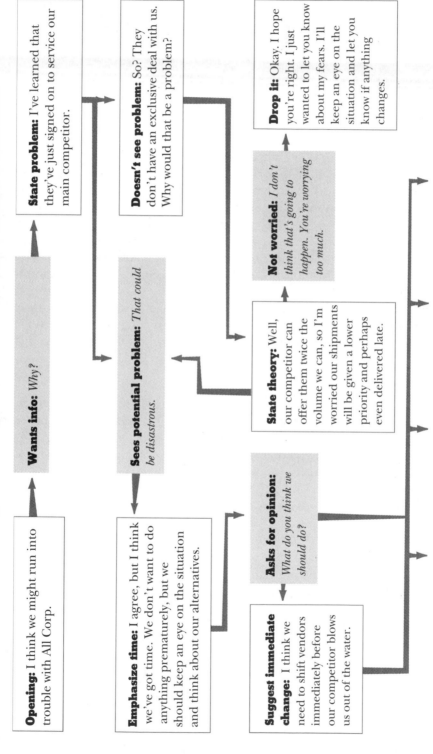

Opening: I think we might run into trouble with All Corp.

Wants info: *Why?*

State problem: I've learned that they've just signed on to service our main competitor.

Sees potential problem: *That could be disastrous.*

Doesn't see problem: So? They don't have an exclusive deal with us. Why would that be a problem?

Emphasize time: I agree, but I think we've got time. We don't want to do anything prematurely, but we should keep an eye on the situation and think about our alternatives.

State theory: Well, our competitor can offer them twice the volume we can, so I'm worried our shipments will be given a lower priority and perhaps even delivered late.

Not worried: *I don't think that's going to happen. You're worrying too much.*

Drop it: Okay. I hope you're right. I just wanted to let you know about my fears. I'll keep an eye on the situation and let you know if anything changes.

Asks for opinion: *What do you think we should do?*

Suggest immediate change: I think we need to shift vendors immediately before our competitor blows us out of the water.

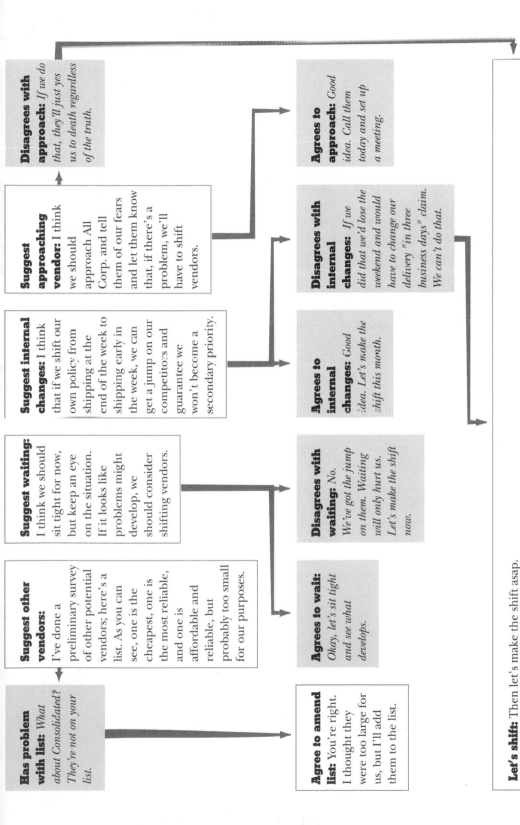

Has problem with list: *What about Consolidated? They're not on your list.*

Suggest other vendors: I've done a preliminary survey of other potential vendors; here's a list. As you can see, one is the cheapest, one is the most reliable, and one is affordable and reliable, but probably too small for our purposes.

Suggest waiting: I think we should sit tight for now, but keep an eye on the situation. If it looks like problems might develop, we should consider shifting vendors.

Suggest internal changes: I think that if we shift our own policy from shipping at the end of the week to shipping early in the week, we can get a jump on our competitors and guarantee we won't become a secondary priority.

Suggest approaching vendor: I think we should approach All Corp. and tell them of our fears and let them know that, if there's a problem, we'll have to shift vendors.

Disagrees with approach: *If we do that, they'll just yes us to death regardless of the truth.*

Agrees to approach: *Good idea. Call them today and set up a meeting.*

Agree to amend list: You're right. I thought they were too large for us, but I'll add them to the list.

Agrees to wait: *Okay, let's sit tight and see what develops.*

Disagrees with waiting: *No. We've got the jump on them. Waiting will only hurt us. Let's make the shift now.*

Agrees to internal changes: *Good idea. Let's make the shift this month.*

Disagrees with internal changes: *If we did that we'd lose the weekend and would have to change our delivery "in three business days" claim. We can't do that.*

Let's shift: Then let's make the shift asap.

ADAPTATIONS

This script can be modified to:
- Warn a superior about a potential personnel problem.
- Warn a superior about a potential client problem.

KEY POINTS

- Be prepared to present alternative responses to the problem.
- Recognize that time is an ally that shouldn't be ignored or relied on.
- Don't discount the possibility that the problem won't arise.
- Emphasize the advantage of taking the time to make the right choice, placing an even greater value on the time you've provided the company.

Apologizing to Your Superior for Your Own Backstabbing

32.

STRATEGY

If you've been badmouthing someone rather than complaining to the individual involved or your boss directly, and you suspect word may get back to your boss, you're best off heading in to apologize before you're called on the carpet. While your undignified and potentially fractious behavior may not be something you're eager to own up to, it's better to face it now than let it come back to haunt you. If you admit your own backstabbing, you'll not only undercut the seriousness of your behavior, but you'll indicate you're aware of your mistake and that it won't happen again. Start by apologizing to the individual involved. Then offer your superior a solid reason for your behavior, even if its just a matter of losing your temper. However, acknowledge there's no excuse for backstabbing. You'll have simultaneously turned yourself in and given yourself a suspended sentence. You may actually come off gaining in your superior's eyes!

TACTICS

- **Attitude:** You are contrite. You've seen the error of your ways. You realize your behavior has had a potentially damaging impact not only on the individual involved but on the company's esprit de corps. Still, you're positive you've cleared the matter up directly and have mended your working relationship. Don't be smug. Emphasize your determination not to repeat your mistake.
- **Preparation:** Assess the extent of the damage before going in to see your superior. How much does she know and how upset will she be? Have a reason (not an excuse) for your actions. Apologize to the individual involved beforehand.
- **Timing:** Do this as soon as you've realized the error of your ways and have had a chance to apologize to the injured party. If you wait for signs the boss may find out, you'll be too late.
- **Behavior:** Nobody likes admitting errors, but be as natural as possible. Present what happened calmly and tell the truth. If it's awkward, say so. If you can't believe what you did, share that as well. Human beings make mistakes. The more human you come across the more likely you'll be readily forgiven.

2.5. Apologizing to Your Superior for Your Own Backstabbing

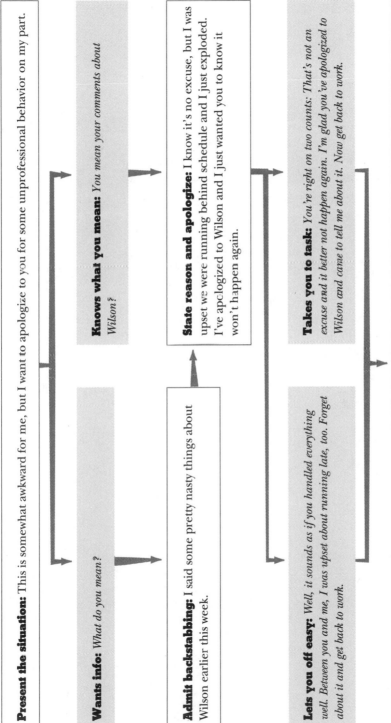

Present the situation: This is somewhat awkward for me, but I want to apologize to you for some unprofessional behavior on my part.

Wants info: *What do you mean?*

Knows what you mean: *You mean your comments about Wilson?*

Admit backstabbing: I said some pretty nasty things about Wilson earlier this week.

State reason and apologize: I know it's no excuse, but I was upset we were running behind schedule and I just exploded. I've apologized to Wilson and I just wanted you to know it won't happen again.

Lets you off easy: *Well, it sounds as if you handled everything well. Between you and me, I was upset about running late, too. Forget about it and get back to work.*

Takes you to task: *You're right on two counts: That's not an excuse and it better not happen again. I'm glad you've apologized to Wilson and came to tell me about it. Now get back to work.*

Express thanks: Thanks for listening to me.

ADAPTATIONS

This script can be modified to:
- Apologize to a superior for poor judgment.

KEY POINTS

- Have a reason, but acknowledge it's not an excuse.
- Be positive about your ability to continue working with the injured party.
- Be prepared either to be let off with a slap on the wrist or to be taken to task, depending on your superior's own past behavior.
- The more human you are in behavior, the more apt you are to be forgiven.

III

Lifescripts

...for Vendors

Asking a Vendor to Lower Her Price

33

STRATEGY

The secret to getting a price reduction from a vendor or supplier is to have an external reason for the request. It can't simply be that you want a higher profit at her expense. The external reason can be anything from a difficult client to an outside auditor or an unfair competitor. Obviously, the more important you are to this supplier, the more likely you are to get a reduction. Similarly, it will be easier if this is a one–time reduction. You can make longer–term reductions more palatable by making them temporary, agreeing to have another discussion at a specific point in the future. Make sure you're speaking with someone who has the power to make such a decision. Also, make sure this request truly is essential for your bottom line. This isn't something you can do regularly when your cash flow gets tight.

TACTICS

- **Attitude:** You're not asking for the vendor to take a loss, simply to lower her profits temporarily to keep your business.
- **Preparation:** The more you know about the vendor's profit margins the better, so do some research. If you find out she has given price concessions to others, your case is strengthened. Also, make sure you've targeted someone with the power to make this decision.
- **Timing:** The best time to do this is either just after you've paid your most recent bill or just after placing a large order at your regular price. The idea is that there will be fresh evidence of your importance to the vendor.
- **Behavior:** It's okay to have this conversation on the telephone. Don't start out with a threat to shift your business. Instead, present it as a favor from one businessperson to another. If that doesn't work, ratchet up the pressure incrementally until finally saying directly that you'll have to shift your business unless the vendor agrees. Agree to any vague request for a *quid pro quo*. It's more of a face–saving gesture than a real request.

3.1. Asking a Vendor to Lower Her Price

Icebreaker: I consider you to be much more than a vendor [or] supplier. That's why I know I can take you into my confidence.

One-shot reduction: I'm doing a project for Acme Cable. They're very tough, as you may have heard. I'm working on a very tight margin on this one and I need your help. I need you to reduce your profit on this one and charge me [desired price].

Ongoing reduction: My bank has been reviewing my lines of credit and my margins. They've told me I have to improve my profitability if I want to keep my credit. To do that and stay in business, I'm going to need your help.

Agrees: I hate to do it, but if this job is that important to you I'll do it. But it's just this once, and you owe me one.

Won't do it: When I deal with you it's always straight. I've always given you my best price.

Can't do it: I've always given you my preferred price. To do any more will only hurt me. I don't think I can help you.

Agrees: You're really killing me, but I don't want to be the one who puts you under. This can't go on forever. In three months we've got to return to normal.

Extraordinary situation: I've never questioned that. But right now I'm involved in an extraordinary situation. I want to stay with you, but I'm going to need your help.

Temporary situation: Look, I really want to keep on working with you. I value our relationship. But I need your help. After the bank is off my back, we can have another conversation.

Agrees: *Okay. If you put it that way, I've really no choice. Remember, what goes around comes around.*

Express thanks: You've got it. Thanks for your help. I'm glad we'll be working together on this.

Can't do it: *I might be out of business by then. I just can't do it. I'm sorry.*

Reconsider: Look, do me a favor. Think about it overnight. I really want to continue working with you. You can get back to me tomorrow.

Can't do it: *I'd like to help you, but I can't commit suicide. I have to sell it to you for the current price. That's the best I can do.*

Reconsider: That means I won't be able to use you for my deal with Acme. Please reconsider. You can get back to me tomorrow.

Agrees: *Okay. If you put it that way, I've really no choice. Remember, what goes around comes around.*

Express thanks: You've got it. Thanks for your help. I'm glad we'll be working together on this project.

ADAPTATIONS

This script can be modified to:

- Make an unusually large purchase from an often used retailer.

KEY POINTS

- Be direct and unambiguous. If possible, make a specific request.
- Make it clear whether this will be a one–time reduction or an ongoing reduction.
- If the vendor agrees right away, however grudgingly, immediately express your thanks.
- If the vendor balks, stress that the situation is either extraordinary or temporary and that you want to continue to use her services.
- If the vendor continues to balk, ask her to reconsider and make it clear that otherwise you'll have to take your business elsewhere.
- If the vendor asks for a vague *quid pro quo*, agree immediately.

Complaining to a Vendor about His Service

34

STRATEGY

It's not uncommon for vendors, particularly consultants who come into your office, to run way behind schedule or to have problems getting things right. Whatever the reason for the unsatisfactory service, it's essential you get the results you're paying for as quickly as possible. You don't need the consultant to become a permanent staff member or to get paid for making mistakes. The secret to getting better service is to have a concise discussion that says you have a problem with the service, and that probes for a reason. Your goal in this dialogue is to get better service, so be prepared to call any bluffs the vendor makes about your staff, to absorb any criticisms he offers, and even to eat a little crow if need be.

TACTICS

- **Attitude:** Be direct and clear. The service is unsatisfactory. You want to know why.
- **Preparation:** Go back to the original plans or proposal the vendor is working from and see if there's been a deviation. Interview anyone assigned to interface with the consultant to find out if there's a problem in–house. Finally, prepare a memo that reiterates your goals and needs.
- **Timing:** Call the vendor to set up a meeting, at your convenience.
- **Behavior:** Hold this meeting in your office. Make sure it's entirely private and confidential. Speak quietly. Make it clear you care about one thing only—getting the job done. Force the vendor to give a reason for the problem, address the reason directly, and tell the vendor to get on with the job.

3.2. Complaining to a Vendor about His Service

Icebreaker: I'm very concerned about the length of time it's taking to get the system operational. I need to get it up and running. If there has been a problem with one of my people, tell me right now. If you're having a problem, then I need you to do something about it, even if it means going out and hiring your own consultant.

Blames your staff: *I know it's taking longer than anticipated, but June keeps giving me conflicting directions. I don't think that she's fully familiar with your requirements or that she has sufficient time to put into this.*

Acquiesces: *I had no idea that you were having more than the average problems. I'll redouble my efforts and if I need any help I'll bring it in.*

Blames you: *Listen. Rome wasn't built in a day. This is a complicated system. You've barely been involved in the process and you've no idea of the problems I've had on this job.*

Remove problem: Okay. If you believe her uncertainty is the reason for the delay, I will remove her from any responsibility. I will sit with her and fill her in on exactly what I want. Or, if you think you can repair your relationship with her, I will free up more of her time.

Provide memo: I'm glad to hear you say that. Just to make sure there's no further misunderstanding, here's a memo spelling out exactly what I want from you.

Take responsibility: If the problem has been my lack of clarity or involvement, I'll accept responsibility. I will no longer be an obstacle to your completing this job as we originally contracted.

Backs down: *I think I can work with her if she has the time to give me and if she's clear on your needs.*

Backs down: *Thank you. Now I feel like we're getting somewhere. I don't think I'll have any further problems.*

ADAPTATIONS

This script can be modified to:
- Complain to a service provider working with your child.
- Complain to a service provider working with your parent.

KEY POINTS

- Be direct and very concise. The meeting should have no digressions—just as the vendor should have no digressions from getting the job done.
- If the vendor blames one of your staff, say you'll either remove the person or take the authority yourself and then insist that the job now gets done.
- If the vendor blames you, accept responsibility, say you won't be a problem anymore, and insist that the job now gets done.
- If the vendor backs off or acquiesces, thank him or her and offer the memo reiterating your needs.

Soliciting a Bid from a Vendor

35.

STRATEGY

This is probably the shortest script in this book, yet it's one of the most important for business people. Very often, faced with having to bid on a very competitive, potentially lucrative project, business people are limited by the profitability of their own subcontractors. One way of landing that big project is to put the pressure on your own vendors to, in effect, become partners with you in the project. The only way this is going to work, however, is if you can hold out the opportunity of a big, profitable pay off down the road. Far–sighted vendors who have the ability to take a chance will be willing to do some initial work at their cost, or even a loss, if it results in a long–term profitable relationship. The secret here is to ask for bids on both parts of the project so the vendor can see that you're not just pushing for a low price. By the way, keeping the name of your own client under wraps could help.

TACTICS

- **Attitude:** Be completely honest and clear about what you need. Don't feel guilty: They're helping you in a marketing effort that will be of long benefit to them as well.
- **Preparation:** If this is a new relationship, make sure the vendor comes highly recommended and is established enough to be able to "invest" with you in a major project. Find out who the decision maker is and speak with him or her directly.
- **Timing:** This dialogue can be held at your own convenience.
- **Behavior:** Have the conversation over the telephone. Be up front about exactly what you need. Let them make their usual statements about how good they are at what they do. Close by reiterating exactly what you expect from them.

3.3. Soliciting a Bid from a Vendor

Icebreaker and pitch: This is Sally of the Jones Agency. You were recommended to me by Sharon Chartling of Acme & Zenith. I'd like you to bid on a printing order. However, before I send you the specs there are a few things you should know about the job. The initial press run on this job is only 5,000 because our client is testing the market. If the test is successful, the press run will be 500,000 monthly. I need a bid on both the test and the full runs. Our client is a large multinational that measures risk very carefully. They want to limit their investment in this testing period to the bare minimum. We're willing to run with them and invest in the concept. We need our subcontractors to make the same kind of investment.

We're competitive: *As I'm sure you heard from Sharon, we're as competitive as anyone in the business and we provide better, more reliable service than any of our competitors. I'm sure you'll be happy with our bid and our work.*

Reiterate: That's why we're calling you to put in a bid. I just need to stress that your bid on the initial run cannot have profit built into it. As for your bid on the rest of the run, we just need it to be competitive. I'll send the specs along. If you have any questions, call me. I look forward to seeing your bid.

ADAPTATIONS

This script can be modified to:
- Ask for any kind of help from a vendor with whom you've had a good relationship.
- Obtain products or services for a charitable organization.

KEY POINTS

- Be very clear about what you need.
- Consider keeping the name of your client from the subcontractor.
- Offer a long–term, sizable, profitable relationship in exchange for a bare bones initial bid.
- Suggest they submit simultaneous bids for both elements: the loss leader and the profit maker.
- Close by reiterating your needs.

Asking a Vendor to Accelerate His Work

36

STRATEGY

Every service you buy from a vendor has four elements to it: speed, quality, scope, and cost. If you're going to request speedier service, you've got to accept that at least one of the other elements must change. In general, it's a mistake to accept a reduction in quality. Therefore, you must be willing either to narrow the scope of the assignment or to increase the amount of money you're paying for it. Be aware that the more advance warning you can give, the less you'll have to reduce the scope or increase the price. Your best leverage in this dialogue is the potential you have to offer additional work, so save that as reward for agreement. Similarly, your biggest stick is taking the assignment away from the vendor, so save that for the final pitch. Avoid getting into detail about the reason for the work to be accelerated. The more details you offer, the more opportunity the vendor has to look for another solution. You've already made that analysis so there's no point in getting them involved.

TACTICS

- **Attitude:** Be clear and concise. Do not apologize—that just lays the groundwork for a price increase. As long as you're willing to up your payment or reduce the scope of the project, you're not asking for anything unreasonable.
- **Preparation:** Exhaust all your other options before going to your vendors. Then, go over the details of the project carefully, looking for ways the scope can be reduced. If you don't find any, be prepared to increase the fee.
- **Timing:** Do this as far in advance of the deadline as possible. The more advance warning you give, the less you'll have to pay as a bonus, the less you'll have to reduce the scope of the project, and the more willing the vendor will be to make changes.
- **Behavior:** You can have this conversation over the telephone. Be single-minded. There should be no hint of the new deadline being negotiable. Deflect initial objections and launch right into your suggestion. Placate fears with the hint of additional work or the threat to take the project elsewhere.

3.4. Asking a Vendor to Accelerate His Work

Icebreaker: I need to speak with you about the project you're working on for me. We're facing a different situation now and I need you to adjust the schedule. It must be done by the 15th and it's urgent.

Can't be changed: *I'm sorry, but my schedule is very tight this time of year and I simply can't get it done by then.*

Sympathetic response: *What happened? What's the matter?*

Sees dollar signs: *Anything is possible. You know that. However, it's going to cost. You're talking about lots of overtime.*

You're resourceful: I appreciate your problem. Because one of the reasons I hired you was your resourcefulness, I think we can work this out.

Vague but firm: Unanticipated outside factors have come up forcing us to move the date up, and there's no option. But I think we can work this out.

You're professional: I knew you'd be able to deal with this. I didn't hire you solely on price, but on your professionalism, too. I think we can work this out.

Suggest reduced scope: I don't think we need to include all original art; canned images would be sufficient. That should cut down the amount of time and minimize the impact on your schedule.

Suggest increased budget: I would have no objection to picking up the cost of your bringing in a part-timer who, under your supervision, could help complete the job on time.

Afraid of costs: *That might work, but how can I be sure this job won't end up costing me money?*

Subtle threat: When I hired you for this job it was with the idea this would be the start of a long–term relationship. If in going the extra mile, you'll be hurt financially let me know and I'll explore other options.

Agrees: *I'm not crazy about it, but I'll do the best I can.*

Hint of future work: I know you never expected this to happen—neither did I. I hope I'll be in a position to express my gratitude in a number of ways.

Afraid of quality: *That might work, but I don't think I'll be able to guarantee the same quality.*

Subtle threat: When I hired you for this job it was with the idea this would be the start of a long–term relationship. If in going the extra mile, you'll be forced to lower your standards let me know. I'll explore other options.

ADAPTATIONS

This script can be modified to:
- Accelerate the work of professionals.
- Broaden the scope of an assignment without significant additional costs.

KEY POINTS

- Be single–minded about the new deadline, but flexible on scope and cost.
- If the vendor reflexively says it can't be done, praise his or her resourcefulness and launch into your suggestion.
- If the vendor reflexively sees dollar signs, show that you're open to negotiation.
- If the vendor probes for details, offer vague answers and your suggestion.
- If the vendor is fearful of costs or quality, threaten to take the project elsewhere.
- If the vendor agrees, offer the vague hope of future projects.

Resisting a Vendor's Commercial Bribery

37

STRATEGY

If you're in a position to approve bids from competing vendors, you're also in position to receive attempted bribes to sway your decision. While the temptation to accept such offers, especially if they come from the vendor you would have chosen anyway, is high, don't succumb. If word gets out that you're corrupt, your reputation and perhaps that of your company will be soiled. The short–term gain you receive isn't likely to offset the long–term impact on your career and company. Rather than reacting indignantly, use bribe offers to your negotiating advantage by taking them as an indication there's room for maneuver. If the vendor insists on doing something for you, ask him to write a letter of praise and send it to your superiors.

TACTICS

- **Attitude:** Don't take the offer personally. It's an indication of neither your reputation nor the vendor's character: It's a sign of how much leverage you have over the vendor.
- **Preparation:** You'll never know when a bribe will be tendered, so you should research your company's and your industry's policies on what is considered an acceptable reward or gift and what is considered a bribe. Standards vary from industry to industry and company to company.
- **Timing:** You have no control over when someone offers you a bribe.
- **Behavior:** Don't be indignant, flustered, or holier than thou. Treat it as a negotiating ploy that failed and move on.

3.5. Resisting a Vendor's Commercial Bribery

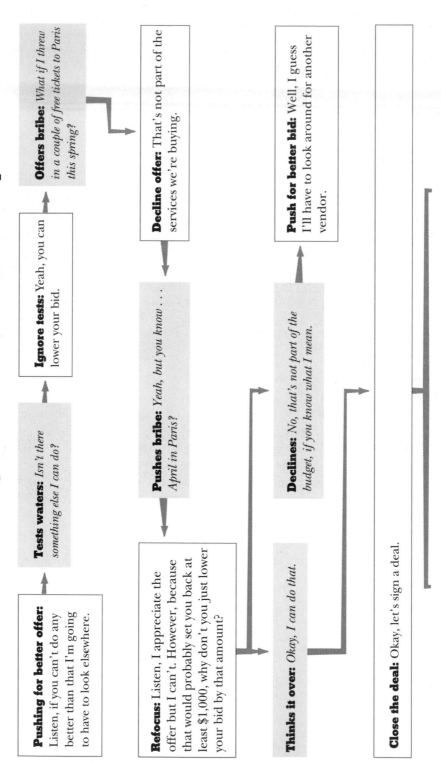

Pushing for better offer: Listen, if you can't do any better than that I'm going to have to look elsewhere.

Tests waters: *Isn't there something else I can do?*

Ignore tests: Yeah, you can lower your bid.

Offers bribe: *What if I threw in a couple of free tickets to Paris this spring?*

Decline offer: That's not part of the services we're buying.

Pushes bribe: *Yeah, but you know . . . April in Paris?*

Refocus: Listen, I appreciate the offer but I can't. However, because that would probably set you back at least $1,000, why don't you just lower your bid by that amount?

Declines: *No, that's not part of the budget, if you know what I mean.*

Push for better bid: Well, I guess I'll have to look around for another vendor.

Thinks it over: *Okay, I can do that.*

Close the deal: Okay, let's sign a deal.

Offers post deal bribe: *You know what, I can still offer you those tickets if you're interested.*

Thanks but no thanks: I appreciate the offer, but no thanks. I'll tell you what you can do, though. Why don't you write a note to my superiors telling them what I great job I do.

Apologizes for bribe: I'm sorry about offering those tickets. It's just that this is a very big deal for the company and I was told to do whatever it took to get the job.

Brush off apology: Don't worry about it. I know its part of doing business. If you want to do something for me, you can write a note to my superiors telling them what a great job I do.

ADAPTATIONS

This script can be modified to:
- Decline any offer on principle and focus discussion on business.
- Say no to anyone who's offering you something you can't accept.

KEY POINTS

- Be prepared for commercial bribery and know your company's and your industry's rules and customs.
- Decline the offer graciously and calmly—don't make it a big deal.
- Use the offer as a chance to gain further concessions.
- If the vendor insists on doing something for you, ask him to write a note of praise.

Threatening Litigation against a Vendor

38

STRATEGY

One of the toughest jobs a manager has to face is putting pressure on a vendor who is tightly tied to the company. In theory, the manager has the right to make demands of the vendor and sue him for non-performance. In practice, it's a bit tougher when the vendor went to school with the CFO, plays golf with the COO, gave the CEO's daughter a trip to Europe as a wedding present, and maintains all of the company's product specs and customer lists on his computer. If you push him the wrong way, the vendor might complain to your bosses. The trick is to make it clear that you don't like lawsuits, but you might have to proceed with a lawsuit to protect both yourself and your bosses from criticism by other parties.

TACTICS

- **Attitude:** Bringing suit against vendors who are in breach of contract is part of doing your job. You are doing the vendor a favor by alerting him to this.
- **Preparation:** Know the contract your company has with the vendor, and be sure he will be in violation of it. Be aware of alternative vendors in case the situation gets sticky. Detail and quantify the costs to your company of the vendor's poor performance. Choose a likely bogeyman: accountant, stockholders, gadfly, auditor, IRS, consultant, possible merger partner, parent company, divorce lawyer, etc. Consult with the company lawyers before using this threat and—this is essential—get advanced clearance from your boss so you don't appear to be a loose cannon.
- **Timing:** Start this maneuver early so you have some room to seem like a good guy when you give the vendor a bit of extra time.
- **Behavior:** Give the vendor a teaser call that you have to talk about something important. Sometimes that alone will be enough for the vendor to take the hint and clear up the problem. Hold the meeting in your office during business hours. Take notes during the meeting to underscore the seriousness of the situation. Do not accept any invitations or gifts from the vendor—not even a pen—from the moment you start this maneuver.

3.6. Threatening Litigation against a Vendor

Teaser call: *Hello, Mr. Gotti. We need to have a business meeting about the cheese shipments. Can you be at my office tomorrow at 3 p.m. for a meeting?*

Opening: Thank you for coming to this meeting. I'm sure you're aware that your shipments to us are are behind. Your trucks seem to have been diverted at times. Now, as part of my job and because we are under close scrutiny from the district attorney, I have to consider taking legal action against you for the breach of contract.

Cites history: *Whoa! Aren't you going a little fast? My family has been in this business for years and no one complains about a little lateness.*

This is the present: I recognize that long history, but circumstances have changed since your family started in the business. We're all under very heavy scrutiny. We work on very narrow inventories, and your lateness is costing us money. Our files have to show that we have done everything we can to stay on time.

Takes offense: *I'm not used to being talked to this way. I think you should show me more respect.*

Not personal: I do respect you. This isn't personal. It's because of that respect that we're talking to you about this now. I am simply doing what my job requires me to do –trying to make sure our contract is honored, so we don't have to answer a lot of questions about why it wasn't.

Threatens to go over your head: *I go back a long way with your boss and I may have to speak to him about this legal nonsense.*

Go ahead: If you feel you need to do that, go ahead. But you should also be aware that I have already spoken with him and he understands that considering a lawsuit at this point is a simple matter of the kind of professional due diligence that the district attorney expects of us.

Asks for leeway: *My family business is going through some hard times right now. Can't you cut me some slack and call off the lawyers?*

Offer limited leeway: I can drop a note into the file and put the matter on hold for one week. If you are not caught up in a week, we'll have to hold this conversation again.